Fisher Investments on Technology

FISHER INVESTMENTS PRESS

Fisher Investments Press brings the research, analysis, and market intelligence of Fisher Investments' research team, headed by CEO and *New York Times* best-selling author Ken Fisher, to all investors. The Press covers a range of investing and market-related topics for a wide audience—from novices to enthusiasts to professionals.

Books by Ken Fisher
How to Smell a Rat
The Ten Roads to Riches
The Only Three Questions That Count
100 Minds That Made the Market
The Wall Street Waltz
Super Stocks

Fisher Investments Series
Own The World by Aaron Anderson
20/20 Money by Michael Hanson

Fisher Investments On Series
Fisher Investments on Energy
Fisher Investments on Materials
Fisher Investments on Consumer Staples
Fisher Investments on Industrials
Fisher Investments on Emerging Markets
Fisher Investments on Technology

FISHER
INVESTMENTS
PRESS

Fisher Investments on Technology

Fisher Investments

with

Brendan Erne
and Andrew Teufel

WILEY

John Wiley & Sons, Inc.

Published by John Wiley & Sons, Inc., Hoboken, New Jersey.
Published simultaneously in Canada.

Library of Congress Cataloging-in-Publication Data:

Fisher Investments.
    Fisher Investments on technology / Fisher Investments with Brendan Erne and
Andrew Teufel.
      p.   cm.—(Fisher Investments Press)
    Includes bibliographical references and index.
    ISBN 978-0-470-45237-0 (cloth)
    1. High technology industries.   2. Investments.   I. Erne, Brendan.
II. Teufel, Andrew S.   III. Title.
    HC79.H53F57 2010
    332.63'22—dc22
                                                            2009041413
Printed in the United States of America

10 9 8 7 6 5 4 3 2 1

Contents

Foreword

Welcome to the sixth in a series of investing guides from Fisher Investments Press—the first ever imprint from a money manager, produced in partnership with John Wiley & Sons. So far, we've also published guides on Energy, Materials, Consumer Staples, and Industrials—four of the ten standard industrial sector classifications—plus emerging markets, a dynamic, diverse region. If you're a serious amateur or a new professional, I encourage you to read them all and I believe you will get at least some benefit from them—maybe a lot.

This guide is on Information Technology—currently about 12 percent of the money value or capitalization weighting of world stocks. Tech may bring to mind awesome TV screens, slick computers, and cool smartphones. But it's also the guts of those products—the bitty brains that make today's tiny phones as powerful as a room-sized computer from just a few decades back. And it's also the IT services that make most firms in other sectors more efficient. If you run a business—any type—you are, in some way, in the technology business.

Many may hear "Tech" and still remember the 2000 Tech bubble. One hot Tech IPO after another in the late 1990s had the world dangerously euphoric, sending stock prices sky high. Eventually, the stock supply from all those IPOs swamped demand, and prices started falling. Tech stocks grinded their way down for three years, then lagged the stock market for years. Some may think Tech is inherently a riskier sector. Not so. Long term, all properly constructed equity categories will have similar returns and similar risks—finance theory says so. All sectors go through periods when they're hot and when they're not. After the period when they're not, the risk is inherently lower.

Tech is, however, fairly economic sensitive—meaning it tends to do better than the market overall when the economy grows robustly, and less well when the economy is sluggish. It makes sense—firms put off upgrading computers and software if they're worried about future profits in a recession. And you might not buy a new laptop—making the old one do for a bit longer. But when the economy turns around, firms need faster, better technology to compete. Better, newer, niftier, and more innovative technology is one of today's business manager's prime tools to get a leg up on competition, or at least ensure you don't have a leg down on them.

But it's not just a matter of hitting economic cycles right—which isn't easy anyway. Some parts of Technology are more elastic than others, and some do better earlier and others later in a cycle. So understanding when Tech and each of its components are more likely to outperform and underperform relative to broader markets—and why—is vital to your success. This book can teach you how.

This book isn't a simple to-do list for picking the "best" stocks, or a primer on timing markets. Such a thing is a fairytale, and any-one telling you otherwise is selling you something for sure—some-thing you not only don't need, but are better off without. Instead, this book and all the books in the series provide a workable, top-down framework for analyzing a sector. It gives you tools allowing you to use commonly available information to uncover profitable opportuni-ties others overlook. And those opportunities can help you to make market bets relative to an appropriate benchmark, with the goal of winning more often than losing. It's a scientific method that should serve your entire investing career. So good luck and enjoy the journey.

Ken Fisher
CEO of Fisher Investments
Author of the *New York Times* Best Sellers
The Only Three Questions that Count,
The Ten Roads to Riches, and
How to Smell a Rat

Preface

The *Fisher Investments On* series is designed to provide individual investors, students, and aspiring investment professionals the tools necessary to understand and analyze investment opportunities, primarily for investing in global stocks.

Within the framework of a "top-down" investment method (more on that in Chapter 7), each guide is an easily accessible primer to economic sectors, regions, or other components of the global stock market. While this guide is specifically on Technology, the basic investment methodology is applicable for analyzing any global sector, regardless of the current macroeconomic environment.

Why a top-down method? Vast evidence shows high-level, or "macro," investment decisions are ultimately more important portfolio performance drivers than individual stocks. In other words, before picking stocks, investors can benefit greatly by first deciding if stocks are the best investment relative to other assets (like bonds or cash), and then choosing categories of stocks most likely to perform best on a forward-looking basis.

For example, a Technology sector stock picker in 1998 and 1999 probably saw his picks soar as investors cheered the so-called "New Economy." However, from 2000 to 2002, he probably lost his shirt. Was he just smarter in 1998 and 1999? Did his analysis turn bad somehow? Unlikely. What mattered most were stocks in general, and especially US technology stocks, which did great in the late 1990s and poorly entering the new century. In other words, a top-down perspective on the broader economy was key to navigating markets— stock picking just wasn't as important.

Fisher Investments on Technology will guide you in making top-down investment decisions specifically for the Technology sector. It shows how to determine better times to invest in Technology, what Technology industries are likelier to do best, and how individual stocks can benefit in various environments. The global Technology sector is complex, covering many industries and countries with unique characteristics. Using our framework, you will be better-equipped to identify their differences, spot opportunities, and avoid major pitfalls.

This book takes a global approach to Technology investing. Most US investors typically invest the majority of their assets in domestic securities; they forget America is less than half of the world stock market by weight—over 50 percent of investment opportunities are outside our borders. While a larger proportion of the world's Technology weight is based in the US, many companies derive a significant portion of profits overseas. Given the vast market landscape and diverse geographic operations, it's vital to have a global perspective when investing in Technology today.

USING YOUR TECHNOLOGY GUIDE

This guide is designed in three parts. Part I, "Getting Started in Technology," discusses vital sector basics, including the history of major developments in Technology. We'll also discuss sector level drivers that ultimately influence stock prices.

Part II, "Next Steps: Technology Details," walks through the next step of sector analysis. We'll take you through the global Technology sector investment universe and its diverse components. The Technology sector itself presents 3 industry groups, 8 industries, and 16 sub-industries. Various firms are driven by enterprise spending, others by consumers, some by infrastructure build-outs. Many are leveraged to combinations of these, yet others are leveraged to none. We will take you through the eight industries in detail, how they operate, and what drives profitability—to give you the tools to determine which industry will most likely outperform or underperform looking forward.

Part II also details many of the challenges Technology firms face, including historical examples of how these challenges have been met and overcome. Moreover, we'll discuss certain products and manufacturing processes used today, as well as how they're advancing through new and emerging technologies.

Part III, "Thinking Like a Portfolio Manager," delves into a top-down investment methodology and individual security analysis. You'll learn to ask important questions like: What are the most important elements to consider when analyzing semiconductor and PC firms? What are the greatest risks and red flags? This book gives you a five-step process to help differentiate firms so you can identify ones with a greater probability of outperforming. We'll also discuss a few investment strategies to help determine when and how to overweight specific industries within the sector.

Fisher Investments on Technology won't give you a "silver bullet" for picking the right Technology stocks. The fact is the "right" Technology stocks will be different in different times and situations. Instead, this guide provides a framework for understanding the sector and its industries so that you can be dynamic and find information the market hasn't yet priced in. There won't be any stock recommendations, target prices, or even a suggestion whether now is a good time to be invested in the Technology sector. The goal is to provide you with tools to make these decisions for yourself, now and in the future. Ultimately, our aim is to give you the framework for repeated, successful investing. Enjoy.

Acknowledgments

A number of colleagues and friends deserve tremendous praise and thanks for helping make this book a reality. We would like to extend our tremendous thanks to Ken Fisher for providing the opportunity to write this book. Jeff Silk deserves our thanks for constantly challenging us to improve and presenting new and insightful questions as fast as we can answer them. Our colleagues at Fisher Investments also deserve tremendous thanks for continually sharing their wealth of knowledge, insights, and analysis. Without these people the very concept of this book would never have been possible.

We owe enormous thanks to Lara Hoffmans for her guidance and significant editing contributions—she was instrumental in completing this book. We'd also like to thank Michael Hanson and Evelyn Chea for their editing work, as well as Evelyn's assistance with citations and sources. Thanks to Dina Ezzat for handling tactical details, and to Leila Amiri for her attractive graphics and images. A special thanks to Brian Kepp, Roger Bohl, Charles Thies, Aaron Azelton, and Brad Pyles for their contributions to data and content. We'd also like to thank Tom Holmes for helping with some of the book's graphics and tables.

Marc Haberman, Molly Lienesch, and Fabrizio Ornani were also instrumental in the creation of Fisher Investments Press, which created the infrastructure behind this book. Of course, this book would also not be possible without our data vendors, so we owe a big thank you to Thomson Reuters and Global Financial Data. We'd also like to thank our team at Wiley, for their support and guidance throughout this project, especially David Pugh and Kelly O'Connor.

Brendan Erne would also like to specifically thank his father Jim, mother Holly, and brother Joel for their ongoing support, as well as his manager John Hulwick for his understanding, patience, and encouragement through the book-writing process.

I

GETTING STARTED IN TECHNOLOGY

TECHNOLOGY BASICS

Technology is a word jammed with meanings. And through the years, it's been philosophized more than you might imagine. Martin Heidegger regarded technology not just as a mechanical process, but a "bringing forth," a ". . . mode of revealing. Technology comes to presence in the realm where revealing and un-concealment take place . . . where truth happens" (319).

Wow! Who knew a simple guide to Tech investing could lead us to the nature of truth itself! Well, we're not going to be quite that ambitious for this book, but it is important to realize technology captures our imagination more than most types of industry. Tech is virtually omnipresent in our greatest hopes and deepest fears about civilization. For every rapturous fantasy we have about flying cars and curing diseases, there are dystopic visions of tech run amok like the Terminator or Darth Vader.

The public has a romantic relationship with technology— sometimes as spiritual and potent as religion. The last years of the 1990s are quintessential—we collectively dispensed with the notion of economic cycles altogether and declared a "new economy" on the wings of savior technology. Conversely, even today we shudder to think of the awesome power of nuclear technology, of robotic soldiers and drone planes—forces seemingly too powerful to control, capable of inducing real Armageddon.

In short, technology carries potent emotional impact—and you'll do well to remember that when investing in it. The romantic vision of technology and successful investing in it are two different matters entirely.

MORE THAN GADGETS . . . A MEANS

Still, context about technology as an idea is important before we go further. Ultimately, a technology is a means to fulfill some purpose. So it may not just be chips or phones or other "gadgets." Technology gets to the heart of human progress. A refined or new math equation is a technology—perhaps a new algorithm suddenly allows a trader to capture and profit from some inefficiency never possible on a derivatives trading desk; or an engineer discovers a simpler, more elegant equation to increase the number of transistors on a microchip, expanding processing power and thus what can be achieved by others still. Both are technologies. Processes are technologies, too—after all, what is software but a process, and what do we call Microsoft's Windows software if not a technology?

Brian Arthur describes technology as capturing natural phenomena and putting them to use. This is done—always—by combination. A new technology is a combination of elements that already exist. That makes tech *recursive*—all devices consist of technologies within technologies. A microchip, for instance, functions as a computer's "brain." But you can break down a chip into its transistors and diodes (all separate technologies in themselves). And you can also trace a chip's functionality all the way down to its most basic features until, ultimately, you get to the basic physics of capturing and manipulating electrical current and conductivity. That is, a chip, at its most essential level, is a use of the phenomenon of electricity toward another end.

Maybe the notion that tech is recursive (technologies within technologies and building on each other) and combinatorial seems obvious, but it's especially important to realize when considering advancements in a larger economy. The elements of anything new must preexist before an innovation (new combination) can take place. We couldn't have a jet plane before we first discovered how flight and aerodynamics worked, or how jet propulsion and fossil fuel combustion worked; likewise, there can't be an Intel 4 Pentium chip until you had the 3 version, and so on. So even a product that seems "brand new" didn't come totally from out of the blue. Apple's iPhone seems totally groundbreaking, but in truth, it merely combines existing cell phone, computer, and touchscreen technologies in a unique way.

In some sense, technologies are never finished—they're always in flux. There are always additions, streamlinings, and new innovations possible. And technologies are never perfect. Generally, a technology must be envisioned first (an engineer or inventor needs to first conceive of what's being created) and executed second. Which means our technologies are not only discoveries of the uses of natural phenomena; they are also products of our minds. And we humans don't tend to produce perfection on the first try. Instead, by iteration, we move forward, improving by increments upon what came before. That's not just true conceptually; it's also true pragmatically in any economy, which has fixed costs and existing infrastructures that can often only handle improvements on existing concepts. For instance, today's PC manufacturers can certainly handle incremental improvements on a new Intel chip—they just adjust the motherboard and it fits right in. But if Intel were to suddenly ditch the semiconductor altogether and offer some kind of new, crazy organic microprocessor that computes on water and algae instead of electricity—well, let's just say Dell would have a tough time manufacturing a computer around such a thing right away.

Over time, revolutions can and do take place—there is little doubt the way we make computers today will be wholly different and barely resemble what we do decades from now. The combinations lead to more and better combinations, ad infinitum, and at an accelerating pace. Revolution via small steps.

Which brings up an important point: We tend to think of tech innovation as faster and faster, smaller and smaller. But that's far too narrow—technology is also about increasing interconnection, efficiency, and opening to new possibilities. New technology creates the potential for ever more and newer things—things we haven't even conceived of yet.

On this broad definition, most things are technologies and technology is in just about everything. In fact, an economy is a kind of technology. Money is one of the greatest of all technologies because it allows folks to trade goods and services more efficiently than any other known mechanism. (Anyway, it's a lot better than trying to deal in clay jars of oil or bartering with cattle, as in olden times.) Stocks and bonds and other tradable securities, too, are tremendous technologies—mechanisms that allow for capital to move ever more efficiently to places of greatest need. Even more, GDP is very much dependent on technology, because growth in productivity happens most often via technological advancement and is thus a huge driver of wealth creation.

But let's not get too excited. This book is for making better investments in technology—correctly forecasting the ways innovation and technology transfer into rising stock prices requires a good dose of discipline and sobriety about these exciting concepts. Many of the greatest innovations and ideas don't translate into company profits for a long time, if ever. For instance, liquid crystal display (LCD) technology has been around for decades, but it didn't become economically viable for mass production as computer monitors and TV screens until recent years. Hundreds of startup tech companies—with seemingly can't-miss ideas—have bankrupted over time. How to pick the right companies at the right times? How can investors quantify a company's ability to innovate via real costs like research and development (R&D) expenses?

These are the sorts of questions this guide aims to address. But first, we need to cover the nuts and bolts of the products the world's largest technology companies make and how they work. After all, to make a disciplined stock investment, an investor must understand the underlying business.

TECHNOLOGY 101

While technology is a broad-reaching term, the Technology sector includes firms that make or distribute electronically based products or services. The opportunity for Technology firms is massive. Firms in every sector and country can invest in technology to help improve the products and services they offer or even make business operations more efficient. For example, a Financials firm may invest in new data storage systems to back up client information. Or it could purchase faster servers to process the data and respond to client needs more quickly. Firms may risk falling behind in the global economy if they don't periodically invest in upgrading their technology—which is why businesses are the leading spenders on technology while consumers are a distant second.

And the global Technology sector encompasses a wide range of firms. When folks think about technology, final products most often come to mind, like the ubiquitous personal computer (PC). Over the last few decades, these machines have made an impressive foray into mainstream society. Not only are PCs necessary for virtually every modern business, they also serve the needs of consumers as entertainment devices, databases, access points to the Internet, and more.

But producing the PC can require the input of many firms across the Technology sector, providing a variety of building blocks like chips, components, and software. Each of these building blocks can come from different companies and regions in the world. Some firms specialize in only one area while others focus on many, and some are purely service based. It's a diverse, global sector.

STARTING SMALL: SEMICONDUCTORS

In order to better understand investment opportunities in the Technology sector, it's essential to first know the basics of the underlying technology itself. And a good place to start is with *semiconductors*. As shown in Figure 1.1, these are manufactured early in the Technology supply chain.

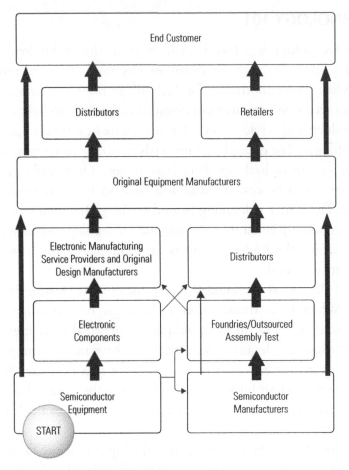

Figure 1.1   Technology Supply Chain

The semiconductor industry is highly complex. In fact, many books can be written on semiconductors and semiconductor equipment alone. Here, we'll provide just a basic outline of the major semiconductor types so in your analysis of the sector you can understand who produces what and why.

But what exactly is a semiconductor? It's a tiny bit of metal that executes orders—sometimes millions of them a second, depending on the complexity of the gadget it's in. There are two basic types— *discrete components* and *integrated circuits* (explained more nearby).

Semiconductors are usually made of silicon—hence "Silicon Valley" in Northern California where many semiconductor firms (designers and manufacturers) are located.

Discrete Components and Integrated Circuits

A *discrete component* contains one active element, like a transistor that simply turns an electrical signal on or off. A *hybrid* can contain more than one active element.

An *integrated circuit* (IC) is a chip imprinted with multiple active elements, like a series of transistors and other electronic or network components that work together to perform various tasks.

Semiconductors, often called *chips*, come in many forms and are one of the first and most important building blocks in manufacturing electronic devices. For example, a PC microprocessor is one type of semiconductor. It acts as the "brain," sending electronic signals that tell PCs to process data.

Types of Semiconductors and End Market Applications

Discrete components are generally less complex—they only contain one active element. A *capacitor* is an example—it is a single component serving no other purpose than storing an electrical charge (which represents the active element). Capacitors are in essence temporary batteries, often found in electronic devices to maintain power in the absence of traditional batteries. Discrete components represent the larger portion of total semiconductor shipments. But because they are simplistic and therefore easier and cheaper to design and manufacture, they sell for a lower price than most other semiconductors.

Integrated Circuits (ICs) are more complex semiconductors with multiple active elements—often an aggregation of many discrete components (hence the term *integrated*). They are sold in smaller volumes, but their higher prices mean ICs make up the lion's share of the semiconductor market. And because they are generally more important to the sector, this section focuses primarily on ICs.

ICs can be broken down into myriad categories, but at the highest level, there are *digital* and *analog* ICs. They are differentiated based on the type of signals processed by the device. A *digital* signal is information coded as discrete sets of numbers (generally binary digits), whereas *analog* is a continuous "real world" signal such as sound, temperature, or voltage. Typical analog semiconductors include power amplifiers and converters. Typical digital semiconductors include microprocessors and memory.

But electronics don't solely use one kind of semiconductor. For example, cell phones have both analog and digital ICs. Speaking into a cell phone creates an analog signal—the voice. The analog IC converts the signal into digital code. This code is processed by a digital IC and sent over the air to the other end of the phone call where it's converted back to an analog signal—the voice heard on the other end.

Analog ICs   Analog semiconductors are a smaller portion of the total IC market relative to digital, but producing them remains a lucrative business. These devices are notoriously difficult to engineer, creating high barriers to entry for the industry. This also means analog designs typically have longer life cycles. Extended life cycles reduce chip manufacturers' urgency to upgrade to the latest and best production equipment, thus lowering development costs. These factors together give analog ICs the highest gross margins in the semiconductor industry.

The analog market can be segmented into *standard products* and *application specific standard products* (ASSP). Standard analog ICs can be used in a multitude of end products while ASSPs are designed for one specific end product. Power management chips, amplifiers, and converters are all standard analog ICs. But these can become ASSPs if modified to meet a certain end product's specifications.

Digital ICs   The majority of the semiconductor market is made up of digital ICs. They're more precise—able to make highly complex calculations. Unlike analog, producing digital chips is hugely capital intensive. Their shorter life cycles relative to analog chips force manufacturers to invest in cutting-edge production equipment to improve and differentiate their products. For example, memory chip manufactures all compete to produce chips on the smallest scale with the largest storage capacity. In order to constantly improve on these metrics, they must invest in the latest and greatest manufacturing equipment. Most digital chips can be broken down into two categories—*logic* and *memory*—logic being the larger market.

Standard *logic* ICs include what could be the most widely recognized semiconductor: the microprocessor. This is an electronic device's "brain" and is most often found in computational machines like PCs, servers, mainframes, etc. *Microcontrollers* also fall into the standard logic space. (Microcontrollers are similar to microprocessors but are used in devices requiring less computational speed and power.) Automobiles, washing machines, and office equipment use microcontrollers. Outside the standard market, there are myriad logic chips with more specific purposes—like application processors, which are basically less powerful microprocessors found in cell phones.

The two most common types of *memory* ICs are dynamic random access memory (DRAM) and NAND (i.e., "not and") flash. DRAM is commonly found in computers and is a form of *volatile memory*—it does not retain information in the absence of a power source. Conversely, NAND flash is a form of *nonvolatile memory*, which retains information without power. NAND is most often found in consumer electronics like cell phones and MP3 players.

End-Market Applications

Once manufactured, semiconductors are shipped to equipment manufacturers in various end markets. The largest end markets are computers and mobile handsets—representing 40 percent and 20 percent of global semiconductor consumption, respectively.[1] The remaining end markets are divided between consumer electronics, industrial applications, automotive, and other forms of communication equipment.

Until 2000, the Americas represented the largest regional consumer of semiconductors. But beginning in 2001, Asia Pacific (excluding Japan, the world's second largest economy) took the lead and, by 2007, made up 48 percent of global semiconductor sales.[2] This dominance was due to the large concentration of electronic equipment manufacturers in the region. In aggregate, this market has grown from only $342,000 in annual sales to over $255 billion in the last 30 years.[3]

GETTING LARGER: PRODUCTS AND COMPONENTS

After development and shipment, a semiconductor is then built into its corresponding final product. This section details products in the computer hardware, communications equipment, and consumer electronics end markets, as well as major components for each.

Computer Hardware

One of the most widely recognized Technology products is the computer or, more specifically, the PC. To the average person, a PC is often used for work, accessing the Internet, storing and playing media files, or writing college term papers. But a PC is only one of many types of computers.

A computer, simply, is a data-processing machine. It follows sets of coded instructions to perform tasks like saving and retrieving files. Mainframes, workstations, and servers are also computers—each is a type of data-processing machine. Unlike simple calculators, computers can be programmed to perform more than one task. At their core is the microprocessor, which interprets and executes various programs allowing them to function. These devices have also given rise to complex storage systems that centralize data.

Personal Computers (PCs) The vast majority of computers today are PCs, and they come in two common forms: desktops and notebooks. Both have similar features and functionality, with the latter being portable. And notebooks are becoming more popular than ever—global shipments of notebooks outpaced desktops for the first time ever in the third quarter of 2008.[4]

PCs come in many brand "flavors," produced by original equipment manufacturers (OEMs) like Hewlett-Packard, Apple, and Dell. But no matter the packaging, they all are made with the same basic components, including the microprocessor, motherboard, memory, hard disk drive (HDD), and liquid crystal display (LCD). (A more detailed overview of these components and their functions is provided in Chapter 6.)

Peripherals   Peripherals are computer hardware depending on the PC to function and usually attached externally (e.g., keyboards, printers, scanners, cameras, microphones, speakers, disk drives).

As separate electronic devices, peripherals typically incorporate semiconductors, circuit boards, and various electronic components and are usually (though not always) produced by the actual PC maker. For example, Hewlett-Packard is a leader in both global PC and printer sales.

Netbooks   A *netbook* is a basic version of a notebook. Smaller in size and with fewer components and software, these devices primarily function as Internet portals. Their limited functionality makes them cheaper (and generally lighter and smaller) than traditional notebooks and a big success in emerging markets. Taiwan's ASUSTeK Computer Incorporated was the first mover with its Eee PC. Since its launch, almost all PC manufacturers have released some form of a netbook.

Workstations   *Workstations* are more powerful desktop PCs—rather like a server with a monitor. But unlike most servers, they're generally not used as a central hub in network environments. Given their higher relative performance over traditional PCs, they're used for more complex tasks like graphic design and modeling.

Mainframes, Servers & Blade Servers   The term "mainframe" has become less prevalent in today's computing world. In fact, mainframes are usually referred to as servers, and only the largest servers are called mainframes.[5] At one point, a single mainframe computer could fill an entire room. But after years of technological advancements, they're now often the size of a refrigerator or smaller.

Servers are vital products in computer hardware, with networking and the client-server model becoming the de facto standard for businesses. As shown in Figure 1.2, the client-server model is a networked environment where individual PCs (the *clients*) are connected to a server. This model allows sharing of information among all networked clients, greater storage capacities (information is saved on servers rather than limited client terminals), easier maintenance, and better security control.

Types of servers vary but all are essentially powerful computers. They're built with many of the same components as personal computers, just more of them and on a larger scale. Some function as application servers, meaning they serve software applications to clients connected to the network. Others function as web servers and

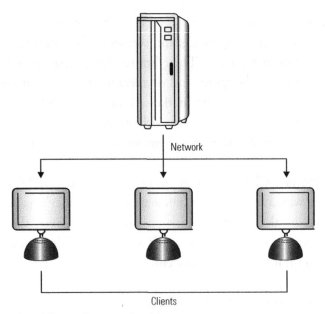

Figure 1.2   Client-Server Architecture

connect clients to the Internet. Because information is viewed on the client terminal, servers do not typically incorporate monitors.

Blade servers are a variation of standard rack-mounted servers. The removable "blades" themselves can be considered computers, with each blade operating independently and made up of different components. Blade servers have been gaining in popularity because of their reduced space requirements, reduced power consumption, and easier physical deployment since new blades can simply be added to an existing chassis.[6]

The Data Center *Data centers*, also known as server farms, are large collections of servers housed in a single environment. They're often built by telecommunications firms and corporations as hubs for network traffic and central computing. Space in these facilities can be leased, leaving management of the data center to a third party. They're classified into four different tiers, as determined by the Telecommunications Industry Association (TIA). Each differs in technology and architecture, with the highest tier generating the least amount of expected downtime in any given year.

A River Runs by It

Data centers can be massive in size. Internet giant Google has built a data center the size of two football fields along the Columbia River in Oregon.[7] The location was chosen partly due to the abundance of hydroelectric power that can feed the facility's significant energy requirements. Data centers accounted for 1.5 percent of total US electricity consumption in 2006.[8]

Enterprise Level Storage Devices and Technologies As of 2008, the size of the digital universe was approximately 281 exabytes, which translates into more binary "1"s and "0"s than estimated stars in the entire universe.[9] All the data need to be stored somewhere, which has led to the rise of large storage systems. *Enterprise level storage devices* are mostly comprised of magnetic disk arrays (HDDs). Depending on capacity requirements, a single system can include thousands of drives.

Communications Equipment

Ever wonder how all those e-mails get from point A to point B? Or how music and video gets downloaded onto cell phones? Communications equipment allows corporations and consumers to form computer networks, connect to the Internet, video conference, or simply chat. While computer hardware performs calculations to generate data, communications equipment allows it to be shared. Products in this market typically fall into three categories: fixed-line infrastructure, wireless infrastructure, and mobile handsets.

Fixed-Line Infrastructure   *Fixed-line infrastructure* is often referred to as *wireline* because physical wires connect end users. For example, a landline phone and most Internet connections use a fixed line. This equipment helps route data between two endpoints, and its history goes back to the invention of the telephone.

Products include routers, hubs, switches, and the physical wires themselves running between each. Globally, most fixed-line infrastructure for traditional voice services has already been built out, so growth in this industry is mostly for the Internet. But to understand how these products work, it's good to grasp the underlying technology.

A major milestone was the transition from circuit-based to packet-based switching. Circuit-based switching opens a line that's all yours until you hang up—like driving on the highway in a lane restricted to everyone but you. But that makes traffic worse for those in other lanes. It'd be better if everyone could change lanes according to how fast they're going, and when and where they need to get off the highway.

This massive inefficiency led to *packet-based switching.* Instead of holding open a dedicated line, information is broken up into small "packets" where it can be intermixed with other data and sent along a shared line. Though more efficient, the problem is ensuring all information gets to the right place after it's broken up.

Routing equipment—hubs, switches, routers—makes this happen. They get information from point A to point B on a network, examining the address attached to each data "packet," forwarding it to the appropriate destination, then reassembling it into its original form.

Hubs are simplest—designed only to receive an incoming signal and pass it on to all other points connected to them. They've more or less been replaced by *switches*, which are more intelligent. Switches can receive an incoming signal and send it solely to the desired destination, rather than all destinations connected to the switch. *Routers* are the most complex, capable of receiving signals of any protocol, identifying the underlying address, and rearranging the data to fit the destination's network protocol before finally forwarding it on.

Cisco Systems is the 800-pound gorilla in this market, serving all types of customers. The Telecommunications industry is a significant buyer, but corporations large and small require fixed-line infrastructure, installing many of these devices in data centers to connect company servers and storage devices to the outside "networked" world.

Wireless Infrastructure   The wireless market is one of the largest industries in the world, and it's still growing. As of this writing, there are over 3.8 billion wireless connections worldwide, with most subscribers concentrated in Asia Pacific[10]—meaning almost 60 percent of people on earth use a cell phone. This gigantic market is primarily divided into two camps based on underlying technology. *Global System for Mobile* (GSM) communications is the most prevalent technology worldwide—over 80 percent of wireless connections use GSM technology.[11] *Code Division Multiple Access* (CDMA) is the leading alternative.

Both standards send digital voice and data information over wireless networks. Newer versions of these technologies are also being implemented (referred to as "third generation" or 3G). Both 3G standards incorporate CDMA technology with Wideband Code Division Multiple Access (WCDMA) stemming from the GSM camp and

CDMA2000 from the CDMA camp. These third generation networks have higher bandwidth, resulting in faster speeds for downloading data or surfing the Internet.

Both standards are built using the same basic equipment—base transceiver stations and antennas (illustrated in Figure 1.3). Together, they make up the cell site, which sends and receives wireless signals as radio waves. Signals received are then transferred to fixed-line networks before being retransmitted wirelessly at the other end (another cell site).

Wireless networks aren't as cumbersome to build as fixed-lines since they don't involve physically laying cables. However, they're extremely capital intensive. Not only is equipment expensive, carriers also must spend heavily on *spectrum*—the amount of airwaves available to offer their services. In 2008, US carriers Verizon and AT&T combined spent in excess of $15 billion for spectrum![12] The spectrum purchased was in the 700 MHz band, which was freed up from the nationwide switch to digital television.

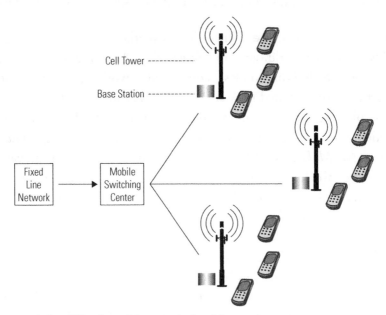

Figure 1.3   Wireless Network Architecture

Telecommunications firms are the primary purchasers of wireless infrastructure equipment. However, they're not exclusive owners of cell sites. In some cases, it can be difficult to establish a new wireless tower due to various environmental and government regulations. In these scenarios, telecommunications firms may lease space on existing towers built by a third party. These third parties typically don't offer wireless services directly, but instead specialize in owning, leasing, and servicing towers.

Mobile Handsets   Mobile handsets are now about as ubiquitous as wallets (and in some countries, they are even used as wallets). Globally, over 1.2 billion mobile phones were shipped in 2008.[13] Mobile handsets are the second largest market for semiconductors behind computers.

Outside of the PC, they have become the most central electronic device in everyday life. They now offer rich multimedia functionality with the ability to store and play video and music, connect to the Internet, synchronize e-mail accounts, act as calendars and day planners, even play video games—the most sophisticated are deemed "smartphones." Mobile handset components are also very similar to a PC—a circuit board, microprocessor, keypad, LCD screen, memory, and power source.

A unique characteristic of the handset market is the extensive use of telecommunications carriers. Most mobile phones are sold to end customers by service providers (e.g., Verizon Wireless, AT&T, Sprint). These firms often pay handset manufacturers a set price, which is then usually subsidized for customers in order to attract new business for their service plans.

Consumer Electronics

Consumer electronics can come in thousands of different forms—televisions, digital cameras, DVD players, car stereos, calculators, camcorders, etc. Sometimes, the defining line between Technology and Consumer Discretionary sector firms is blurry. Outside of mobile handset manufacturers, if a firm specializes in purely consumer electronics it will typically be classified as Consumer Discretionary. However, consumer electronics play an important role in the Technology sector. These goods can be sold directly by Technology firms or drive demand for Technology components.

Televisions   Televisions are a sizeable portion of the consumer electronics market. Cathode ray tube televisions, or CRTs, have historically been the de facto standard but are increasingly being replaced by flat panel displays like LCDs. In fact, televisions are one of the largest drivers of LCD demand, along with notebook and desktop PC monitors.

Video Game Systems   Currently Nintendo's Wii, Microsoft's Xbox 360, and Sony's PlayStation 3 are the dominant video game systems. Over the past few decades, these machines have become increasingly sophisticated and fueled demand for more advanced microprocessors, graphic chips, memory, and other components. Just like cell phones, video game consoles are becoming similar to PCs in components and functionality. All three consoles even include Wi-Fi chips for connecting to the Internet. While not as large as PCs, the market for these devices is still capable of influencing demand for parts and components across the technology supply chain.

MAKING IT ALL WORK: SOFTWARE AND SERVICES

So far, this chapter has detailed hardware components and products. But all this hardware is useless without one critically important element: software. What good is a hard disk drive if a computer doesn't know how to access information stored on it? Without software, a PC is just a very expensive paperweight—it's not possible to access e-mail, connect to the Internet, play a DVD, or type a term paper without software. Software is the instructions, or code, telling the hardware how to function and interact with other hardware and the end user.

Another differentiating feature between hardware and software is the distribution model. Software has no physical building blocks—it's simply code. It doesn't require semiconductors and electronic components to develop (other than the PCs used to write the code). In fact, the vast majority of input costs are R&D. Software can be preinstalled on hardware during the manufacturing process or installed after the hardware's final purchase. Sales range from prepackaged (think Microsoft Office in retail stores), to enterprise-wide licenses or even seat-based licenses (for businesses). Under the licensing model, there are generally fees for updates and maintenance. Some software can also be downloaded directly to hardware via the Internet.

Software comes in myriad forms, but we'll discuss the following:

- Operating systems
- Application software
- Middleware
- Internet software

Operating System

Think of *operating system* (OS) software as similar to the microprocessor. It's the core set of instructions and simply tells hardware how to operate. PCs, servers, workstations, cell phones, and video game systems all have operating systems. The OS can provide system management, communication to hardware and networks, file access, and a user interface (UI).

Microsoft Windows is perhaps the best-known OS—it's nearly ubiquitous across the global PC market. Its defining feature is a unique UI allowing users to perform tasks in separate graphical "windows."

OS software varies by the product it's used in. For example, Unix is a standard most often used in high-powered computers like servers and workstations. Sun Microsystems' Solaris is one of the more popular Unix-based operating systems used today. Linux operating systems, very similar in design to Unix, are found more in servers than traditional PCs. Their unique open source software is free and not patented by any one firm. This enables them to be altered and customized at will.

Application Software

Application software is designed for a specific task. For example, Microsoft's widely used Office suite includes Outlook, Word, Excel, and PowerPoint—all application software. There are applications for security, client relationship management (CRM), and enterprise resource planning (ERP). Apple's iTunes is another application software, allowing users to access and manage music libraries. The possibilities for application software are infinite and depend only on the ability to imagine new tasks to perform.

Middleware

Between the OS and application software lies *middleware*. While a user can see the OS and application software through their corresponding UIs, middleware is behind the scenes. It's responsible for providing interoperability between different software programs. The benefits can most easily be seen in networked environments, which typically consist of hardware running on multiple operating systems. Middleware translates programs from one operating system to fit the format and/or protocol of another. Many operating systems and application programs now come with already built-in middleware.

Internet Software

Search engines represent the largest market within Internet software. The software performs highly complex algorithms to generate lists of websites best matching (according to the search engine's unique criteria) whatever keyword is entered. Google, Yahoo!, and Microsoft are the largest three search engine providers in the US. But Internet software isn't limited only to search as any web-based application can fall into this market. Web browsers, Internet retail, and travel applications all use Internet software.

IT Services

With so many different forms of hardware and software, it can be difficult for businesses to effectively manage IT systems. IT services firms specialize in systems integration, consulting, business process outsourcing, and payment and transaction processing. Other services include custom programming and software development. These businesses are global in scale, with operations in hundreds of countries.

Offered by hardware manufacturers, software providers, and independent firms, these service offerings can help businesses run more efficiently and maintain focus on their core areas of expertise. For example, a bank with no significant IT expertise would be more inclined to hire a third party to process account transactions. This is likely less costly than hiring a large team of IT professionals to develop the software internally.

Chapter Recap

You've now been introduced to some of the fundamental characteristics of the Technology sector. We will build upon many of the concepts presented in this chapter as we progress into later chapters.

- The Technology sector is highly diverse, consisting of a wide gamut of semiconductors, components, products, software, and services.
- Globally, technology plays a vital and necessary role in everyday life. Enterprises, which account for the vast majority of spending, must invest in technology to stay competitive. Consumers also account for a substantial portion of spending, which is more discretionary in nature.
- Semiconductors are the basic building blocks for electronic components and products—computers and mobile handsets represent the largest end markets.
- Hardware can come in many forms, but ultimately software enables it to function.

2

A BRIEF HISTORY OF
MODERN TECHNOLOGY

Technological advancements abound through history and helped push civilization forward—sometimes faster, sometimes slower—to greater wealth and better health. From cavemen mastering fire and using rocks as tools, to movable type, the Industrial Revolution, radios, light bulbs, cars, and microchips—all were mind-bending break-throughs in their time and paved the way toward further innovation and technological advancement.

Like the Industrial Revolution, the last decades have heralded a new historical turning point: the Information Age. This is a period of instant and near unlimited proliferation and access to information—a modern-day renaissance where information is sought and shared freely. But how did it come to be, and what might it mean for investors? Good, informed investing decisions often require the context of history. No, you don't need to become an expert on the history of technology, but it's worth taking a stroll through the past to see where we've been to get a sense of where we may go.

Semiconductors, computers, communication devices, and the Internet all played a role fostering the Information Age. This chapter details a brief history of their development. It also covers the build-up to the 1990s Tech bubble, how it burst, and its aftermath.

THE SNOWBALL EVENT: HISTORY OF SEMICONDUCTORS

We'll start with chips. Sure, it would be great fun (and maybe a bit tiresome) to begin with the wheel as the first technology and work all the way up to today, but as investors we're more concerned with the more relevant history of today's investible technologies. Without semiconductors, there would be no cell phones, computers, or Internet—no Intel, Microsoft, Hewlett Packard, Oracle, or Apple! Semiconductors are the bedrock foundation for much of today's technology—among the first and most important building blocks in manufacturing electronic devices. Their development is one of the most important milestones on the road to the Information Age. But where did semiconductors come from?

Eureka! A Half-Way Conductor!

In 1833, natural philosopher Michael Faraday stumbled upon the first known "semiconductor effect" while investigating the impact of changes in temperature on silver sulfide.[1] He noticed the metal's conducting power increased with heat and fell when heat dissipated. This contradicted the known effects of temperature on other metals. We know now this is a property of most semiconductors. An interesting discovery, but what do you do with a metal that gets more conductive the hotter it gets? Not much, until you discover rectification and transistors.

Rectification is when electrical currents flow in a single direction—a basic but vital effect to functional electronic devices. It was discovered in 1874 and its first broad application was detecting radio signals in the early 1900s.[2] This is a classic feature of many technologies—a principle is discovered but may not become applicable in a mass (or profitable) way until years later. Around the same time, silicon entered the picture. An engineer with American

Telephone and Telegraph (now AT&T) tested rectification on thousands of minerals, with silicon crystals and germanium performing better than others.[3]

Building on earlier work from John Bardeen and Walter Brattain, William Shockley of Bell Labs first conceived the junction transistor in 1948. The transistor could be used to switch and amplify electrical currents—another task vital to electronic devices and one previously performed by vacuum tubes. A major benefit over vacuum tubes was the transistor's much smaller size—which has only gotten smaller over time. Early transistors were made with germanium, but silicon emerged as the material of choice due to lower electrical leakage and ability to withstand extreme temperatures.[4]

The Transistor Transition

The first commercially successful product incorporating transistors was the radio.[5] Hearing aids were also early adopters. Because these products needed to be portable, transistors were more attractive than larger vacuum tubes, despite the initial high cost of production.

The Dawn of Integrated Circuits

As electronics grew more complex and required thousands of transistors, interconnecting them became increasingly difficult. In the search for an easier solution, integrated circuits were born in 1958. This breakthrough is credited to two individuals: Jack Kilby of Texas Instruments and Robert Noyce of Fairchild Semiconductor. Integrated circuits (ICs) were a giant leap forward in the development of electronic devices. Instead of producing a single transistor at a time, multiple transistors and components could be built on a single piece of semiconductor material. This enabled more automated manufacturing and the ability to produce smaller and more powerful chips. However, producing these powerful chips was cost prohibitive.

Initial Applications

Defense was one of the few markets where the benefit of an IC's small size outweighed its high cost of production. The US Air Force used ICs in computers and Minuteman missiles in the 1960s. But the potential for integrated circuits was much greater. Prior to ICs, electronics like computers and calculators were made with vacuum tubes. This hindered the devices' wide-scale adoption because vacuum tubes are much bulkier. A single computer could be as large as an entire room. ICs allowed electronics manufacturers to scale down size and overcome these limitations.

In following years, ICs increased in complexity and functionality. This move was driven by economics: Unit costs fell as the number of components per chip increased[6]—getting more bang for your buck, so to speak. It was during this time that former Intel CEO Gordon Moore observed the number of components on an IC doubled roughly every two years—now referred to as "Moore's Law."

A Giant in the Making

In 1968, Robert Noyce and Gordon Moore left Fairchild Semiconductor to start a new company with approximately $2.5 million in funding. Originally called NM Electronics for "Noyce Moore," the two purchased rights to use another name—Integrated Electronics, or Intel for short.[7] At the time, Intel focused primarily on memory, intent on making chips practical for mass adoption. They also wanted the best-performing and most reliable products on the market.

Research and development (R&D) and economies of scale became vital cornerstones of successful semiconductor firms. The industry is characterized by rapid technological advancement—firms need to invest heavily in R&D or their products risk becoming obsolete. Production costs were equally important. (What good is the best chip on the market if no one can afford it?) Intel recognized this and, to this day, R&D and economies of scale remain two of its core strengths—it is now the largest semiconductor manufacturer in the world.

The Microprocessor

1971 was another breakthrough year. Intel went public and launched the world's first microprocessor—the 4004. The Intel 4004 had the same computing power as the 1946 ENIAC—the first electronic computer built.[8] Produced on a two-inch silicon wafer, this single chip contained 2,300 transistors and all parts for a working computer.[9] Though the chip was designed for a calculator, it was fully programmable. Functionality could be customized with different software, allowing use in myriad electronic devices.

Intel's success led to new iterations of the microprocessor, sparking a revolution in computing devices, including the personal computer, but also creating competition. Over the next decade, Fairchild Semiconductor, Texas Instruments, RCA, Motorola, IBM, and Advanced Micro Devices all manufactured microprocessors. By the end of the 1970s, a saturated market led to price wars—an environment favoring those with best economies of scale.[10] Recognizing the need to lower production costs, Intel was the first to move production overseas in 1972. It also took a unique approach and built massive chip manufacturing plants, which lowered unit costs relative to competitors operating smaller facilities. This helped Intel with one of its greatest victories—being chosen as the microprocessor supplier for IBM's PC in 1981. Its chips weren't superior to competitors', but they could be made at lower costs.

Rise of Japan and Asia

By the 1980s, Japan had invested heavily in semiconductor production. Focused on memory, the region excelled at producing high-quality chips through finely tuned manufacturing processes. Japan gobbled market share and, by the middle of the decade, surpassed the Americas in semiconductor billings. This almost bankrupted Intel, forcing the firm to sell a portion of itself to IBM in 1982.[11] It also led Intel to exit the memory business in 1985 and focus solely on microprocessors.

But Japan's reign began to fade. By the early 1990s, PCs were penetrating further into businesses and homes, and Intel was a primary beneficiary. Its economies of scale and R&D in the microprocessor market were unrivaled. But a new region was on the rise—Asia, particularly South Korea and Taiwan, was investing in chip production with a focus on memory. Using Intel as an example, Asian companies departed from Japan's strategy of superior quality and placed a stronger emphasis on cost. Asian manufacturers began mass producing memory and were able to take market share from Japan. As seen in Figure 2.1, Asia surpassed Japan in aggregate semiconductor billings by the late 1990s and even surpassed the Americas by the early 2000s.

Another competitive advantage Asia had—the cost of building a manufacturing plant and employing labor was significantly lower than in the US and Japan. Some firms, such as Intel, saw this and opened international production facilities. This also led to the creation of out-sourced third-party semiconductor manufacturers domiciled in Asia.

The New Millennium

Relative to previous years, semiconductor advancement over the last decade has been less dramatic. R&D will continue to play an important role in the industry. However, the incremental performance benefit of

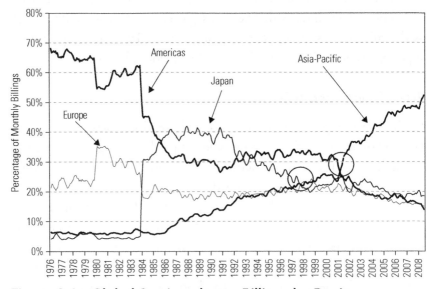

Figure 2.1   Global Semiconductor Billings by Region
Source: Thomson Reuters.

new ICs is less significant today than it once was. In other words, current microprocessors are powerful enough for software that hardware improvements are not as noticeable to users. This makes low cost structure ever more critical.

Advancement has primarily been through manufacturing processes. One such example is the transition from 200mm to 300mm wafers. The larger size allows more chips to be produced on a single wafer. Another is the increasing number of transistors crammed onto chips by shrinking feature sizes (Moore's Law). Both these trends can improve production scale, and those able to make the transitions faster have enjoyed advantages over peers.

Microprocessor Multiplier

Following the release of the first microprocessor in 1971, Intel's 4004, the number of transistors has increased at a dramatic pace. The 4004 held 2,300 transistors. Today, an Intel quad core chip produced at the 45 nanometer level contains about 800 million transistors.[12]

HISTORY OF COMPUTERS

The computer, one of the most important inventions of the last century, has a history and timeline intimately intertwined with semiconductors since breakthroughs in semiconductor technology made today's computers possible. Computers are now small, smart, fast, and everywhere—but how did we get from the abacus to the ultra-skinny laptop?

Early Origins

A computer's function is simply to make computations. By this definition, calculators were technically early iterations. But the earliest machines we'd understand as true computers in the pre-integrated circuit days were huge because of bulky vacuum tubes. They were just too big for mass adoption. Deemed the first "computer," the ENIAC, built in 1944, contained almost 18,000 vacuum tubes, weighed 30 tons, and filled an entire room.[13] It was supposed to calculate military artillery firing tables, but the war ended before it could be completed.

Many of the early computers were developed for government and defense purposes, simply because the government was one of the few customers who could afford them. But the discovery and ongoing development of ever smaller and cheaper integrated circuits allowed computers to be developed as general purpose machines, leading to wider adoption.

Big Blue

In 1952, Thomas Watson, Jr. was elected president of a firm called IBM, which specialized in timecard equipment. He led the transition from timecards to computers, and in 1959, IBM released its first set of transistorized computers. The company's focus on superior technology and aggressive pricing tactics made it difficult for competitors to gain market share, and, by 1961, it's estimated IBM held over 80 percent of the computer market.[14]

IBM took a risk in 1964, developing the System/360—computers with interchangeable software and peripherals—a significant departure from the existing industry model of large, all-encompassing mainframes. Demand was strong.

But tides began turning in the late 1960s. Part of IBM's initial success was its ability to bundle the System/360 products since it sold individual machines at much higher prices. This backfired when customers were ready to upgrade components and did not want to pay for entirely new bundles. It created an opportunity for competitors to offer cheaper IBM-compatible equipment—eventually forcing IBM to lower prices to maintain leadership.

The PC

In the 1970s, smaller "personal" computers were springing up. Companies like Apple, Northgate, Zenith, ZEOS, Atari, and Commodore were all in the market, while IBM, who failed to identify the trend early, lost market share. The firm turned itself around in 1981 with the IBM PC. Superior distribution and service made the PC an instant success and industry standard. The PC's small size and lower price point blew the market wide open, leading to widespread adoption by enterprises—its intended target market. It was even cheap enough to enter homes. A marked change from IBM's previous vertically integrated approach, the PC used third-party components, running on an Intel microprocessor and Microsoft's MS-DOS operating system.

Man of the Year?

The "personal computer" was so successful that *Time* named it the 1982 Man of the Year. In an article titled, "The Computer Moves In," *Time* states its reason:

There are some occasions, though, when the most significant force in a year's news is not a single individual but a process, and a widespread recognition by a whole society that this process is changing the course of all other processes. That is why, after weighing the ebb and flow of events around the world, Time *has* decided that 1982 is the year of the computer. It would have been possible to single out as Man of the Year one of the engineers or entrepreneurs who masterminded this technological revolution, but no one person has clearly dominated those turbulent events. More important, such a selection would obscure the main point. *Time's* Man of the Year for 1982, the greatest influence for good or evil, is not a man at all. It is a machine: the computer."[15]

Attack of the Clones

Success of the IBM PC made it a benchmark for imitators, and in the 1980s myriad firms produced IBM PC-compatible computers. Because each PC was built with similar off-the-shelf parts, the industry became increasingly commoditized. Superior hardware and software were no longer differentiating factors. Offered at lower prices, clones eroded IBM's market share and the firm lost its lead in PCs.

Apple emerged as a major player during this time and released the Macintosh in 1984. Instead of running applications on coded instructions, the "Mac" incorporated a graphic user interface (GUI). The GUI used icons and windows—this user-friendly approach helped with its success. But despite innovative technology, Apple kept its software and hardware design proprietary and charged a premium over competitors. With no low-cost compatible alternatives, it failed to become an industry standard like the PC.

A New Revolution in PC Manufacturing

While businesses and consumers rapidly adopted PCs in the 1990s and the market matured, a firm called Dell emerged with a unique strategy. Instead of charging a premium for superior products, Dell focused on service and cost management. The firm cut out middlemen and shipped products directly to customers. It built customized computers to order, improving customer service and reducing costs since there was little in-process inventory.

Dell's supply-chain management strategy was remarkably successful and helped establish it as the world's leading PC manufacturer—a distinction it traded with Hewlett-Packard (HP) on occasion. (HP took the lead in 2006 and has maintained it since.) Dell's core market was in desktop computers, particularly in the mature US market. The firm failed to gain a strong enough presence in emerging markets and in notebook computers—the two largest growth drivers in recent years. These, however, were areas of strength for HP, allowing them to gain market share.

Upgrade Cycles

Computer technology evolved rapidly, but demand had less to do with new PC models and more to do with the goods inside. The two largest drivers historically were new generations of microprocessors and software, specifically operating systems.

Role of Microprocessors Intel's rise as the globally dominant manufacturer of microprocessors was partially aided by their scale and R&D, but marketing was perhaps equally as important. You may recall their "Intel Inside" branding campaign, launched in 1991, which successfully enlightened the public on the importance of the microprocessor in their computer. This direct marketing approach was previously used by PC manufacturers, but it was new for component manufacturers.

Differences between microprocessor generations in the 1990s were more significant than today. The benefits of increased speed and efficiency outweighed the cost of upgrading—and when coupled with Intel's successful advertising, demand for PCs would usually increase with each new generation of processors.

Role of Software   Evolving software also impacted demand for new computers. The IBM PC used MS-DOS as its operating system, but Microsoft retained licensing rights. This meant PC-compatible manufacturers could adopt MS-DOS to mimic the IBM machine as best as possible. The rapid growth of these compatibles quickly established Microsoft as the industry standard.

Under Bill Gates' guidance, Microsoft released many iterations of its operating system. The first version of Windows came out in 1985 and was similar to Apple's Mac OS. Its GUI used icons and tiled windows to display applications. Newer versions were released in following years, and, like microprocessors, demand for PCs would increase because updated operating systems often required more robust hardware.

HISTORY OF COMMUNICATIONS

Most investors today easily understand why mobile phones and related equipment fall in the Technology sector rather than Telecom. Today's phones aren't really phones—they're credit card-sized powerful computers you can use to retrieve and send e-mails, store contacts, manage your schedule, write a doctoral thesis, play games, and, oh yes, talk. But how did we get from smoke signals to bulky Princess phones to super cool tiny "gotta-have-'em" handhelds?

Mobile Phones

Personal mobile phones made their entrance in the 1970s but were primarily for experimental and trial purposes. The first known cellular phone call was made in 1973 by Dr. Martin Cooper of Motorola, who set up a base station in New York and called his longtime rival at Bell Labs.[16] It wasn't until the early 1980s that the technology was launched commercially in the US. Motorola was first to the game in 1983 with its DynaTAC mobile phone—the size of a brick—boasting one hour of talk time and eight hours of standby.[17]

Other mobile phones were springing up internationally from Finnish and Korean giants Nokia and Samsung. These revolutionary devices cost thousands of dollars and were too cost prohibitive for the mass market.

Battle for the Top

The 1990s set the stage for what are now the big five in mobile phones: Nokia, Samsung, LG Electronics, Motorola, and Sony Ericsson. While still somewhat expensive by today's standard, the cost of cell phones and wireless service was falling, and they were on their way to becoming ubiquitous in the developed world. Nokia and Motorola were the dominant players during this time, each with a unique strategy.

Finland's Nokia made an early strategic decision to focus on telecommunications. It shed other business lines and built a vast distribution and manufacturing network. This generated economies of scale still unrivaled today. Cost had become its core strength. The firm used this to its advantage in competitive pricing environments to gain market share over peers. By 1998, Nokia became the world's leading mobile phone manufacturer, a title it still holds today.[18]

Motorola was a strong competitor with a different strategy. A pioneer in the mobile phone market, innovation was at its core. In the cell phone industry, smaller is generally seen as better, and Motorola consistently beat peers to market with innovative and smaller models. In 2004, the Motorola RAZR set the standard for slim phone design and became one of the world's best-selling handsets ever.

However, the firm grew overly dependent on this phone and failed to release compelling new lines. Its previous strength became its weakness, ending in heavy market share losses.

Smartphones

The definition of *smartphones* has changed over time, but it generally refers to phones with more advanced features—and higher price tags. Many early versions were personal digital assistants (PDAs), but their popularity faded as traditional cell phones began offering similar features. Nokia made an early entrance into smartphones in the mid-1990s and, to this day, is the world's largest provider.

However, this lucrative market attracted new entrants. Research in Motion (RIM) developed a unique service allowing users to synchronize corporate e-mail to its secure business servers. This led to significant market share gains, particularly with business customers. Apple is another, albeit more recent, newcomer with its iPhone. This popular touchscreen device put Apple on the smartphone map almost instantly. Its success led almost every major phone manufacturer to release a similar touchscreen handset. It also demonstrated that a non-traditional handset manufacturer could penetrate the market, encouraging more new entrants from other industries.

HISTORY OF THE INTERNET

The Internet is both the result of, and an important ingredient in, further fomenting the Information Age. It's hard for most folks today to remember a time when memos weren't delivered instantly and information wasn't readily available 24/7—all from your desk, lap, or telephone. How did we get from those barbaric not-so-long-ago days to the 24/7 wired days?

Early Origins

The Internet's origins trace back to the 1960s and the Advanced Research Projects Agency (now Defense Advanced Research Projects

Agency, or DARPA). Commissioned by the US Department of Defense, this agency created ARPANET: A network of computers connecting US universities and research institutions. It used packet switching technology and interface messaging processors (IMPs), basically modern day routers, to share information—small amounts of it, slowly, and with frequent interruptions.

"E-mail," such as it was, was developed in the 1970s, but even more important was establishing the transmission control protocol/Internet protocol (TCP/IP) as the standard method for interfacing. Developed by Robert Kahn and Vint Cerf, this allowed computers and networks of various kinds to communicate with one another—a kind of universal language and the same protocol used today.

Commercialization

In the mid-1980s, the National Science Foundation (NSF) developed the NSFNET for faster communication between research and academic institutions. It was designed to be a "network of networks" that would also connect to the ARPANET.[19] However, non-restricted academic access led to significant traffic growth the NSFNET could not support. As a result, the NSF solicited bids to upgrade the network, and the winning proposal came from IBM and MCI.[20] The private sector was now involved.

Managing the network, however, was cumbersome as there were vast amounts of information in different forms. This made it challenging to organize and find data. Tim Berners-Lee found a solution in 1989. While working at the European Organization for Nuclear Research (CERN) in Switzerland, he proposed a hypertext markup language for transferring information over the Internet. It was a vast improvement from the previous system, and he called it the World Wide Web (WWW).

Recognizing a better browser was necessary for navigating the Web, the team at CERN started looking for outside help. A group of students at the University of Illinois responded with a program called Mosaic. The user-friendly browser grew in popularity and was later released for PC and Macintosh computers. This quickly led to widespread adoption of the World Wide Web. By 1994, there were 10 million Web users on 10,000 servers, a fifth of which were commercial.[21] The Information Age kicked into high gear.

The Dot-com Era

Conditions in the mid to late 1990s were ripe for growth. Demand for Internet access was rapidly increasing and Web business opportunities were plentiful. To accommodate the significant rise in demand for Internet service, there was also a period of heavy infrastructure investment. Sales of copper and fiber optic cables, routers, switches, and computers increased. This period helped bolster demand for hardware and software alike, leading to a broad rise in Technology stock prices. There were points when the Technology sector represented over one-third the weight of the S&P 500 Index.

The Boom

Infrastructure suppliers were initial beneficiaries of the Internet boom. The physical network needed to expand if businesses and consumers were to gain access. It began when the NSF commissioned private firms to build Internet access points. Controlled by WorldCom, Pacific Bell, Sprint, and Ameritech, these points were designated for public use.[22] However, they couldn't handle the increasing amount of network traffic and additional infrastructure was needed. This came from large telecommunications firms like AT&T that built out their own private Internet access points. In attempts to attract businesses, many cities across the US also built out extensive fiber optic networks.

Demand for routing equipment skyrocketed during this period. Cisco Systems was the dominant supplier. Founded in 1984, Cisco had an early jump on networking technology. Over the years, it invested heavily in R&D and consistently produced industry-leading products. It also adopted an acquisition strategy in the early 1990s that diversified its product portfolio, making it a one-stop shop for virtually all network communications products. The firm generated $714 million in annual revenue in 1993, which increased to $22.3 billion by 2001.[23]

Internet service providers (ISPs) were next in line to benefit. Demand for access was growing fast. There were approximately 160 US commercial ISPs in early 1995, increasing to about 4,000 by mid-1997 (including Canada).[24] In this increasingly crowded market space, some even offered free service as the battle transitioned from profitability to market share.

Then came the dot-coms. Rapid proliferation of Internet service into businesses and homes opened a whole new channel of opportunities. Firms were offering business to business (B2B), business to consumer (B2C), and consumer to consumer (C2C) web-based services. There were literally thousands of startups, and many of today's most prominent Internet companies (e.g., Google, Amazon, eBay) were started in the 1990s. As detailed in Figure 2.2, the Technology sector was producing more IPOs than any other.

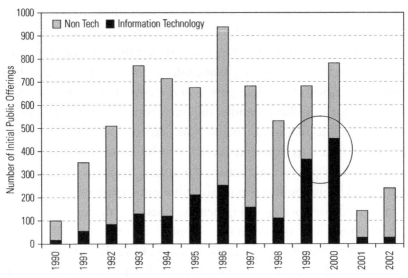

Figure 2.2   Initial Public Offerings: Technology Sector vs. Non-Tech Sectors

Source: Bloomberg Finance, L.P.

Benefits of the rapidly expanding sector weren't solely confined to Technology. Rapid proliferation of new innovative businesses and technology helped bolster the entire economy. Semiconductors, computers, mobile handsets, and the Internet improved efficiency in business and communications. This led to significant productivity gains, with US labor per hour increasing 2.75 percent annually from 1995 to 2000—nearly double the pace of the previous 25 years.[25] Moreover, the 1990s were characterized by one of the longest economic expansions in US history.

The Bust

The party eventually ended as many fledgling firms lacked viable business plans. Focus was placed on share gains through heavy marketing, technology investment, and expansion—all of which required significant capital. The firms couldn't generate enough revenue to cover expenses, burned through cash, and eventually went bust. Webvan is a notable example. This online grocer went public in 1999, raising $375 million in its IPO. It quickly expanded into eight US cities and made a $1 billion order for a group of warehouses.[26] Unable to pay its expenses, the firm went out of business in 2001, less than two years after going public. Hundreds of other Technology firms in the late 1990s shared similar fates.

Valuations across the sector reached astronomical levels on massively euphoric sentiment. Many investors believed Technology's run was only beginning. Many would increase relative portfolio exposure on "dips," claiming they were excellent buying opportunities. The sector generated above-average returns for years, leading investors to "chase heat." In March 2000, the Technology bubble finally burst. Internet companies fell by the wayside, creating sympathy selling throughout the sector.

The Aftermath

The MSCI World Technology sector represented almost 24 percent of the broad index in March 2000, but by March 2003, Technology's share fell to 11 percent.[27] When the dust finally settled, it was clear only the strong survived. Firms with poor business strategies were gone—acquired or liquidated. However, some firms with sound strategies were gone, too—simply recession victims.

The bust also helped shape business strategies over the following years. Historically, many Technology firms had large cash balances to protect against the sector's typical volatility. The bubble bursting and the ensuing recession took this volatility to an entirely new level as demand fell drastically. Numerous firms shifted to more conservative business strategies by increasing reserves and sitting on cash. This worked to the sector's benefit in recent years as global credit markets froze and liquidity dried up. Many sectors were starved for capital, but Technology firms were in a healthier position, able to make acquisitions, buy back shares, or simply weather the downturn. In fact, Technology reclaimed its spot from Financials as the largest S&P 500 sector in May 2008.

Chapter Recap

Semiconductors, computers, cell phones, and the Internet all helped foster the Information Age. Their development has allowed data to be searched for, accessed, and shared almost instantaneously. Along with other factors not discussed in this chapter, these devices have made the Technology sector one of largest single contributors to global productivity gains in recent decades.

- Semiconductor advancement was the spark leading to the technology revolution. Within the industry, successful firms like Intel became dominant through superior R&D and economies of scale.
- IBM played a critical role in the development of modern PCs, but its dominance was tested as the industry became increasingly commoditized. PCs were no longer differentiated through hardware and software, making cost an important factor to successful manufacturers.
- Motorola has long been a pioneer in mobile phones, but Nokia's unrivaled economies of scale have helped it maintain industry leadership. The rapid growth of smartphones in recent years is fueling new market entrants.
- The Internet began as a US government project that grew into the World Wide Web with the help of Tim Berners-Lee. Its development fueled the 1990s dot-com bubble, which eventually burst on stretched valuations and unsound business strategies.

3

TECHNOLOGY SECTOR DRIVERS

In this chapter, we'll outline some of the most important macro-drivers for the Technology sector. There are three broad categories of drivers you can use to examine the forward-looking prospects for any stock market sector:

- Economic drivers
- Political drivers
- Sentiment drivers

We'll start by assessing the economic drivers most applicable to the Technology sector. While much of this discussion will center on the US, the principles can be applied to any country.

ECONOMIC DRIVERS

Macroeconomic indicators take the pulse of the economy. Whether it's jobs numbers, GDP, or inflation readings, they help paint a picture of the current state of the broad economy. And they can help you shape expectations about the economy and how it may impact Technology looking forward.

Deciphering economic data isn't easy. Economic reports can be volatile, contrast one another, and are often subject to later revisions. And economic data are usually inherently backward-looking—the data report on what just happened in the past quarter or year; they don't tell you what's likely to happen in the future. Markets discount economic news with astounding speed, so investors don't need to know what just happened—they must consider what's next.

So how do you use macroeconomic data to your advantage? By staying abreast of the most important indicators and asking whether present conditions are better or worse than reflected in investor sentiment and market prices. Then, consider where you think the economy is likeliest to go in the future based on current trends. You're looking for predictive value. You're not as interested in what's on the cover of the *Wall Street Journal* today. You're interested in what's going to be on the cover next month or next year.

While a full book could easily be devoted to economic drivers, this section will focus on the macro- and microeconomic drivers most applicable to the Technology sector. And, of course, we can't detail every driver. Here we'll cover just those we view as most impactful, including:

- Economic growth
- Fixed investment
- Consumer spending
- Component shipments
- Inflation
- Share supply
- Innovation & upgrade cycles
- Exchange rates

Understanding these important factors can help you determine which Tech stocks to choose and when to hold them in your portfolio.

Economic Growth

Technology is highly *economically sensitive*—it's more likely to outperform during periods of economic growth. And the best way to measure economic growth is a country's gross domestic product (GDP).

What Is GDP?   GDP has four primary components:

1. Personal consumption expenditures: Consumer spending.
2. Gross private domestic investment: Business spending.
3. Government consumption expenditures and gross investment: Spending by federal, state, and local governments.
4. Net exports: Exports less imports.

US GDP measurements are released quarterly by the US Department of Commerce's Bureau of Economic Analysis (BEA, www.bea.gov). In aggregate, GDP represents the final value of all goods and services produced in the US.

Figure 3.1 shows relative performance of Technology versus US stocks and GDP growth. (In other words, if US stocks returned 10 percent in a given year, and Technology stocks returned 30 percent, that's 20 percent relative outperformance.) Historically, Technology tracks closely with the direction of GDP growth—meaning Tech is likelier to outperform when GDP grows.

The lion's share of Technology demand has typically come from developed regions. However, emerging markets are a growing percentage of aggregate Technology spending, so it's important to follow the GDP outlook for these regions, too.

Industry Factors   While Technology is economically sensitive, the relationship isn't black and white—you must analyze economic impact on Technology's discrete industries. Industries can perform differently based on which stage of the business cycle they're leveraged to. Determining whether it's early or late in the expansion can help refine forecasts and improve accuracy. For example, the Semiconductor Equipment sub-industry is one of Technology's most economically

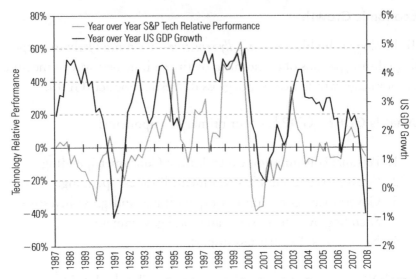

Figure 3.1   S&P 500 Technology Relative Performance vs. US GDP Growth

Source: Global Financial Data, Thomson Reuters.

sensitive areas. It tends to perform best after the aggregate *book-to-bill ratio* (see nearby box) has bottomed. Figure 3.2 shows the ratio can trough multiple times during expansionary periods. However, the deepest troughs have historically occurred in contraction just before the start of a new expansion (as shown in Figure 3.2).

Book-to-Bill Ratio

A ratio representing the number of equipment orders a company receives versus the number of orders it can deliver and bill for. This ratio can be found on the website of global industry association SEMI: www.semi.org.

Figure 3.3 shows a typical economic cycle—contraction through expansion. Because chip manufacturers scale back production and reduce equipment expenditures during contractions, a prolonged period

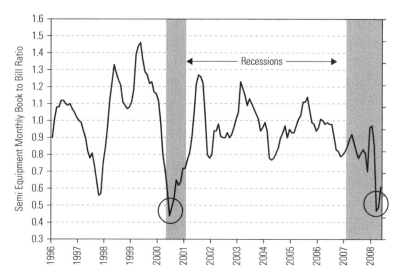

Figure 3.2   North America Semiconductor Equipment Manufacturers Book-to-Bill Ratio
Source: Bloomberg Finance, L.P.

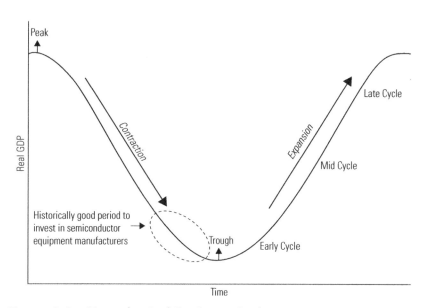

Figure 3.3   Hypothetical Business Cycle

of underinvestment spurs new equipment orders once demand rebounds and expansion begins. Hence, a larger weight in Semiconductor Equipment stocks *before* the cycle begins can increase the probability of outperformance. (This same concept can be applied to other areas of Technology, which will be discussed further in Chapter 9.)

Fixed Investment

Fixed investment can have different meanings, but in Technology, it refers to IT spending by the enterprise market—computers, network equipment, servers, etc. Hardware sales are more economically sensitive and typically rebound earlier during expansion, so tracking fixed investment is critically important.

The US publishes fixed-investment data in quarterly GDP measurements released by the BEA. The report breaks investments down further into computers and peripheral equipment and software. While both are worth tracking, fixed investment in computers and peripheral equipment has historically been a better indication of when Technology will more likely outperform.

Figure 3.4 shows Technology outperformance tracking final sales of Computers & Peripherals equipment closely. However, it's also worth noting periods of underperformance. These tend to occur just before sales growth slows, because the market anticipates the downturn. Simply: Periods of strong fixed investment can help Technology outperform, while weak fixed investment can be a drag.

To help forecast the direction of fixed investment, it's critical to look at the sector's largest end markets—financial services, manufacturing, and communications, for example—which account for 21 percent, 18 percent, and 10 percent of global IT spending in 2008, respectively.[1]

The Financials sector leads the pack for obvious reasons—these firms must store, process, and access massive amounts of sensitive data. Personal client information, account tracking, and transaction processing are all done electronically. As these firms grow they must invest in storage devices, PCs, servers, software, routers, and network equipment.

Manufacturing is more diverse than Financials since it crosses many sectors—Industrials, Energy, Materials, Consumer Discretionary,

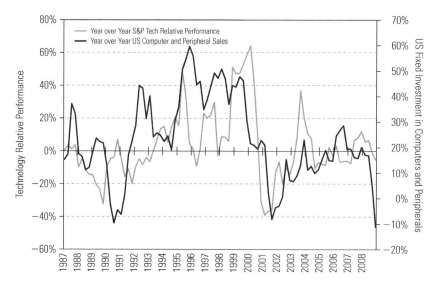

Figure 3.4   S&P 500 Technology Relative Performance vs. US Fixed Investment in Computers & Peripherals Equipment
Source: Global Financial Data, Thomson Reuters.

etc. Over time, technology has made manufacturing increasingly complex, fine-tuned, and efficient. In general, increasing manufacturing levels and capital expenditures translate into stronger IT spending within this vertical.

The communications industry is another big spender—fixed-line and wireless networks both require significant amounts of infrastructure. Equipment is needed to power networks, monitor performance, and manage and maintain traffic flow. To stay competitive, players must invest heavily in technology, so capital expenditure patterns of larger communications firms figure into larger fixed-investment trends.

But again, fixed investment tends to slightly lag Technology outperformance. This means one should consider overweighting Technology if *future* spending in these markets is *expected* to increase. Keeping tabs on guidance from top industry players can help in this effort.

Consumer Spending

Consumers don't technically make fixed investments, but they are significant purchasers of technology. Instead of spending on giant servers and expensive consulting services, they spend on PCs, cell phones, and consumer electronics. And the two largest drivers of aggregate consumer spending are income and employment levels. Very similar to fixed investment, overweighting Technology *before* consumer spending rises can increase the probability of generating more favorable results.

Rising Incomes   As an economy grows, aggregate income levels tend to follow. In most world regions this leads to stronger consumer spending. Some of this spending will be on actual Technology products—a new computer, cell phone, or MP3 player. But even spending on non-Technology items—automobiles, clothes, new homes, even financial products—indirectly impacts Technology because it leads to higher spending by manufacturers (a large end market for Technology products).

Low Unemployment   Low unemployment generally goes along with strong economic growth. As profitability increases, many businesses seek further growth opportunities, which can increase labor demand. Coupled with rising incomes, this creates a perfect environment for robust consumer spending.

Component Shipments

Components are the bits and pieces, odds and ends of hardware used to build working final products like computers, mobile handsets, and televisions. These include semiconductors, hard disk drives, and LCD panels. They're one of the first building blocks in the technology manufacturing chain, so shipments tend to rebound early in the business cycle.

This makes the Philippines an area of focus since electronics are its primary export, totaling 58 percent of the nation's total exports in 2008.[2] And those electronics exports are mostly basic level components— semiconductors and hard disk drives. Figure 3.5 shows that, historically, the Technology sector generally outperformed during periods of strong or increasing Philippines electronics exports. Put another way, it's generally considered better to be overweight Technology when

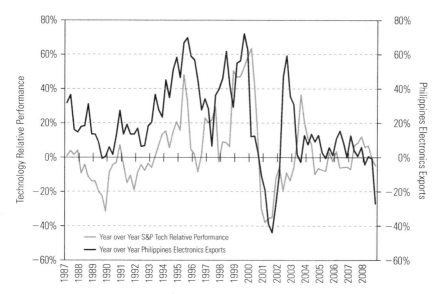

Figure 3.5   S&P 500 Technology Relative Performance vs. Philippines Electronics Exports
Source: Global Financial Data, Thomson Reuters.

shipment growth is strong. There are many forces working on stocks all at once, meaning no single indicator should be used for buy and sell decisions. However, if this indicator were being used in combination with many others, it typically gives a positive (overweight) signal when shipment growth increases to 13 percent or more and a negative (underweight) signal when growth falls below 13 percent. As shown, this rule is not particularly helpful prior to the mid-1990s when there was minimal outsourcing to the Philippines.

And, while this relationship seems intuitive, it's always worth testing. Figure 3.6 shows year-over-year change in *global* discrete device shipment and relative performance of the Technology sector. As in the Philippines example, Technology outperformance has typically tracked strong or increasing discrete device shipments.

Inflation

Inflation, specifically, sharp *disinflation* (a slowing in the rate of inflation), can be a positive Technology driver. Broadly speaking, Technology firms

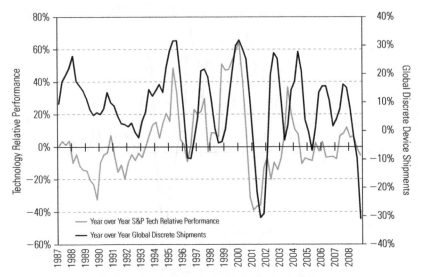

Figure 3.6   S&P 500 Technology Relative Performance vs. Global Discrete Device Shipments
Source: Global Financial Data, Thomson Reuters.

are volume monetizers, not price monetizers. Consider Technology's unique nature: Most of the sector's products are in a never-ending state of *deflation*—prices fall over time. For example, for certain equivalent-capacity notebook hard disk drives, prices fell by approximately *20 percent in the first half of 2007 alone*.[3] While this is an extreme example, most Technology products follow a similar directional trend. This means Technology firms must constantly improve productivity and establish economies of scale to maintain profit margins—a task that becomes significantly easier when inflation slows.

The Core PPI Finished Goods Index represents a good gauge of input prices for Technology firms. Figure 3.7 shows Technology's relative performance as well as growth in Core PPI Finished Goods. Technology outperformance has typically followed sharp declines in PPI growth. A potential explanation for this relationship is the *substitution effect*. As other goods fall in price, consumers and businesses can purchase more discretionary Technology products. Based on this relationship, it is considered better to overweight Technology when year-over-year PPI growth falls below 2.3 percent.

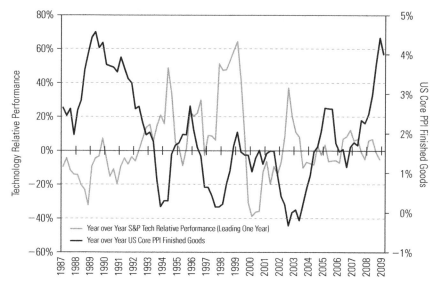

Figure 3.7   S&P 500 Technology Relative Performance vs. US Core PPI Finished Goods

Source: Global Financial Data, Thomson Reuters.

Share Supply

Supply and demand is a basic, broadly applied economic concept—increased supply leads to lower prices, constrained supply to higher (holding demand constant). But few apply this fundamental concept to stock prices. Initial public offerings (IPOs), secondary offerings, stock option issuance, and mergers financed with newly issued shares all increase supply—bearish for stocks. Conversely, share repurchases and cash-based acquisitions decrease aggregate stock supply and can be bullish—whether on a sector level or for broader markets.

This was clearly illustrated during the Technology IPO boom during the 1990s. By 1999, over half of the 685 US stock IPOs came from the Technology sector—a number that increased another 40 percent in 2000.[4] The total value of these IPOs in 1999 and 2000 was approximately $29 billion and $38 billion, respectively. Moreover, many Tech firms infamously issued massive amounts of stock options to employees as compensation. Share count skyrocketed, making each one less valuable. Coupled with a lack of viable business plans, equity supply became unsustainable and the "bubble" eventually burst. The cycle didn't end, however. On the way down, many Tech firms were bought or went bust. This reduced oversupply and helped set up the sector for future stock price appreciation.

Innovation & Upgrade Cycles

The Technology sector is characterized by constant innovation and upgrade cycles where research and development is paramount. Most often, these innovative ideas or technologies come from narrow, focused areas. However, every now and again a new technology or product has the ability to drive broad demand and thus performance across the aggregate sector. History provides some examples.

Innovation   Outside of the personal computer, one of the greatest recent innovations is the Internet, which fundamentally shifted the way society and businesses function. While it existed for many years, wide-scale adoption didn't occur until the 1990s. During this time, demand for Internet access skyrocketed, which in turn helped drive performance across the aggregate Technology sector.

Why did the Internet have such broad impact on the sector? Before consumers and businesses can access the Internet, infrastructure is needed. This bolsters demand for wiring, routers, switches, and powerful computers to manage network traffic. Then, users must purchase Internet-capable computers. Not only does this boost hardware and software demand, but computers are the single largest end market for semiconductors. Chip producers begin expanding to meet demand, which drives sales of semiconductor equipment. This chain of events is a large reason why the period is often called the "tech boom."

Upgrade Cycles   Upgrade cycles are another form of innovation, though not in the sense described previously. Rather, these are driven by newer, "updated" derivatives of existing hardware, software, or components. Over time, various cycles exerted sizeable influence on Technology performance.

The Pentium microprocessor in the 1990s is a good example. Performance enhancements in each new generation were significant, leading consumers and businesses to continually upgrade their PCs. Those upgrades drove further demand for hardware, software, and components.

Another example: Microsoft Windows has generated multiple upgrade cycles. Since its creation, the operating system has been broadly used by both consumers and businesses. And almost every subsequent release has almost instantaneously become the industry standard. Most require more robust hardware to run properly. As a result, Windows releases historically have typically spurred demand for new PCs—which of course then bolstered demand for semiconductors and components and helped drive aggregate Technology performance. The effects of both Pentium- and Windows-driven upgrade cycles on computer sales are shown in Figure 3.8. As illustrated, not every upgrade cycle drove computer sales higher—the Pentium 4 had little effect since it didn't deliver much incremental benefit to

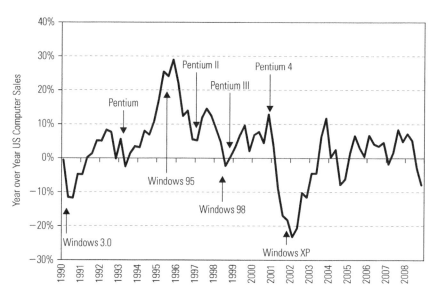

Figure 3.8   US Computer Sales Growth & Upgrade Cycles
Source: Thomson Reuters.

consumers. Windows XP, however, reaccelerated growth, mainly because of its stability and better compatibility with corporate network environments relative to predecessors.

Product support is another factor in upgrade cycles. Most software companies offer product support services in the event of problems. This is especially important in the enterprise market. No company will pay thousands, if not millions, of dollars for software without some form of quality guarantee. However, as new products are released, the cost of supporting older products eventually becomes uneconomical and the firm ends the service. Technology firms can influence their customers to upgrade products and services by phasing out support for older models.

Exchange Rates

Though Tech has a big US concentration, it is a fully global sector. It's not atypical for firms to derive more than half their sales from foreign markets. As such, currency movements can contribute to sector performance. (For our purposes, because the US represents the largest weight in the Technology sector, we'll focus on the US, though global studies might yield different results.)

Figure 3.9 shows US Technology relative performance and year-over-year percent change in the US dollar versus a trade-weighted foreign currencies exchange rate. The US dollar versus foreign currencies scale has been reversed to better demonstrate the correlation. It certainly is not as strong as some of the previous relationships, with a breakdown in the 1996 to 1997 range. However, there are multiple periods when a weak or weakening dollar has coincided with US Technology outperformance.

On a relative basis, weak dollar environments make US products relatively cheaper in international markets, which can help bolster demand. Moreover, when US-based Technology firms repatriate earnings, there is the added foreign exchange benefit of converting a stronger currency into a weaker currency. Money flows may be responsible for periods where this relationship does not hold. The dollar tends to rise as money flows increase to the US, and foreign money tends to

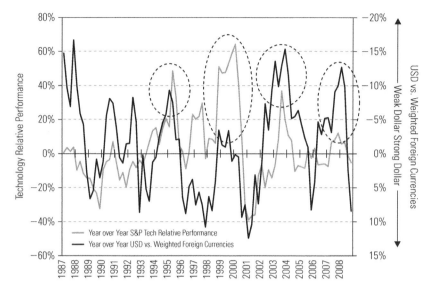

Figure 3.9   S&P 500 Technology Relative Performance vs. USD/Trade-Weighted Foreign Currency Exchange Rate

Source: Global Financial Data, Thomson Reuters.

gravitate toward mega cap companies where there is a disproportionate amount of Technology firms. This likely explains the breakdown from 1996 to 1997, when Technology's status as the "hot" sector outweighed the impact of a strong dollar.

POLITICAL DRIVERS

Government policies are used worldwide to stimulate or slow down growth, protect self-interests, or simply generate tax revenue. Ultimately, political policies mean a shift in money and/or property rights from one group to another. Who wins in the political shell game can impact not only broad markets, but specific sector performance as well. Some of the political drivers most relevant to the Technology sector include:

- Taxes
- Intellectual property rights
- Trade policy
- Industrial policy

Taxes

Tax policy is capable of materially impacting any company. Simply, the more a firm pays in taxes the lower its earnings, and vice versa. But aside from broad sweeping tax policies that affect all sectors, it is important to examine factors more specific to Technology.

Foreign Income Treatment   Many Technology firms today have both domestic and foreign operations. Because product prices tend to fall over time, scores of manufacturers have shifted production to lower-cost regions. These international operations are subject to the local tax code of the country where they're located. But parent companies, again mostly concentrated in the US, face *repatriation* taxes—funds brought back into the US from a foreign subsidiary are often subject to additional taxes. As such, it's likely the sector would react negatively if the US government forced corporations to repatriate funds or significantly raised repatriation tax rates. This would be a bearish driver.

Capital Gains   Capital gains rates also play a role. In general, Technology firms pay less to shareholders in the form of dividends relative to other sectors, leaving higher proportions of retained earnings. Since retained earnings are subject to capital gains, lower rates provide an added boost. For example, in the third quarter of 1997, rates were lowered from 28 percent to 20 percent in the top bracket and 15 percent to 10 percent in the lowest bracket. While other factors were also at play, the Technology sector outperformed the broader S&P 500 Index by more than 40 percent for seven straight quarters (rolling 12-month returns starting in Q4 1998).[5]

R&D Tax Credits   Innovation is central to Technology. In fact, the "Software and Internet" industry ranked highest in 2007 research intensity at 13.6 percent, followed by Health Care at 13.4 percent.[6] (Research intensity refers to the amount of money firms spend on R&D as a percentage of sales.) Given Technology's heavy R&D

spending, any associated tax policies can impact the sector. R&D tax credits have existed in the US (and other countries) for years. The credits are relatively small and, to date, have not had much impact on larger players. However, if these credits were expanded, it would likely be bullish for Technology.

FASB Rule 123R

While certainly important to monitor, tax changes do not always supersede other factors. FASB Rule 123R is a testament to this fact. Originally enacted in 1995, the rule was amended in December 2004, requiring companies to expense employee stock options at "fair value" on the income statement. Prior to this date, option expenses were detailed in pro forma (informal) income statements in footnotes. The net impact was a reduction in taxable income and aggregate taxes payable for companies issuing options. However, it also reduced earnings. Other factors were at play, but this likely contributed to Technology's underperformance in 2005.

Intellectual Property Rights

Intellectual property rights are one of the most critical components of capitalism and properly functioning free markets. Without well-protected property rights, firms have little incentive to innovate or take on new projects. Why would Company A spend millions developing a new widget if Company B could copy and sell the exact same widget for cheaper? A lack of property rights, or even weak property rights, eliminates financial incentives tied to innovation.

While individual governments are responsible for local enforcement, global intellectual property rights standards are set by the World Trade Organization (WTO). Note the word "standards"—these are guidelines, not rules. However, changes in these standards and/or country-specific laws can certainly drive Technology.

Technology companies rely on strict enforcement of property rights to protect products, be it hardware or software. Currently, the WTO dictates that patents are expected to last a minimum of 20 years.

But if this minimum number of years were dramatically lowered, that could be a potentially significant bearish driver for Technology. Hence, monitoring changes in property rights can be an important step in determining when to overweight or underweight the Technology sector.

Real-Life Property Rights

As much related to Telecommunications as Technology, *net neutrality* has been a hotly debated issue for years. The idea is the Internet should be "free" from restrictions on content, downloads, or even connection speeds, among other things. Proponents want laws to ensure these conditions are met. Opponents claim a problem doesn't exist.

Telecommunications firms are the primary opponents of net neutrality because they own most of the "pipes" that carry Internet data. These firms say it's reasonable to charge customers higher rates based on connection speed or the amount of bandwidth used. However, many net neutrality advocates argue telecommunications firms don't have the "right" to price their services this way. They claim the Internet should be an open forum where users can download any content and visit any website without interference from service providers.

At its core, this is a property rights issue. If the government were to increase regulation, the property rights of Telecommunications firms would diminish. This would likely negatively impact the Telecommunications sector's fundamental and stock performance. However, it could help certain Technology firms. Content providers like Google use significant amounts of bandwidth and are net payers to Telecommunications firms for infrastructure usage.

Trade Policy

Another relevant driver to any global sector is international and domestic trade policies. The accommodativeness and/or restrictiveness of policies often depends on the country and specific products being traded. These laws can provide unfair advantages to some firms and sectors and disadvantages to others, and they can have a sizeable impact on overall sector performance.

A Deeper Look at Trade

The Information Technology Agreement (ITA) is a free trade agreement signed under the World Trade Organization. Originally created in December 1996, the ITA is a pact between various countries—its goal is eliminating tariffs on information technology products. It essentially covers computer-related products and office equipment like fax machines and phones. That means corporations from Japan or China can sell their products in the US without having to pay a tariff. Likewise, companies in the US can sell their products abroad tariff-free (obviously, this applies only to participating nations).

The agreement originated with 29 signatories, including Australia, Canada, Japan, Singapore, and the US, to name a few. In order to take effect, the ITA needed to incorporate at least 90 percent of world trade in information technology products, a stipulation that was reached by the April 1997 deadline.[7] The first round of tariff cuts was in July 1997, and the ITA now incorporates close to 40 nations.[8]

It is a shining example of the benefits of free trade, and it represents one of the most successful agreements in recent history. But despite all its success, it has grown outdated. Recent years have given rise to a wide array of new products and technologies. It is concerning that none have been added to the ITA. Many countries still use import tariffs to help protect their domestically produced goods—an inefficient practice that needs to be eliminated to encourage free trade.

Industrial Policy

The last political driver we'll discuss is government spending. Depending on the country, government spending can have a sizeable impact on Technology demand. Many spend heavily in the areas of defense and communications, but some even spend for public use. For example, to offer nationwide broadband access, multiple countries in Southeast Asia have subsidized network buildouts. Spending initiatives like these significantly impact Technology demand. If large enough, future government spending could be a significant bullish Technology driver.

SENTIMENT DRIVERS

Sentiment is the least tangible sector driver. Most simply, sentiment can mean how receptive people are to buying or selling stocks—and like any mood, sentiment can move fast. It plays a large role in near-term market prices because the stock market is driven by humans making decisions—inclusive of their rationalities and irrationalities. The key is identifying which will be most important to the sector looking forward. But some significant sentiment drivers historically—and ones likely to be impactful in the future—include *beta* and *professional market forecasters*.

Beta

Through most of Technology's existence, investors have considered the sector a "high beta" play. In other words, during broad market up-trends, Technology is expected to rise more than the overall market, and during downtrends, Technology is expected to fall more. Over time, this has indeed proved true. The Technology sector has a beta of over 1.7 relative to the S&P 500 over the last 10 years and a beta of 1.3 over the last 6 (to remove bubble years)—the highest of any sector over both periods.[9] This is likely due to the sector's economically sensitive nature. Remember, the market is a *leading indicator* of future economic conditions. Investors generally believe periods of economic strength will benefit Technology more than the broader market, and periods of weak growth will disproportionately hurt Technology. Hence, Technology tends to move in the same direction as the broader market, though with bigger swings.

Beta

Beta is a measure of an asset's performance relative to a chosen market. A beta of 0 means it's not correlated; a negative beta means it's negatively correlated; and a positive beta means it is positively correlated. But unlike simple correlations, beta provides a sense of magnitude. For example, a beta of 1 would imply the asset tends to rise by 10 percent when the chosen market rises by 10 percent. A beta of 1.5, however, would imply that the asset tends to rise 15 percent for every 10 percent rise in the chosen market. Relative to the S&P 500, Technology has been the highest beta sector with respect to monthly returns over the last 10 years. A summary is provided in Table 3.1.

Table 3.1 Sector Betas Relative to S&P 500 Index

Information Technology	1.73
Consumer Discretionary	1.09
Materials	1.07
Telecommunication Services	1.04
Financials	1.04
Industrials	0.99
Energy	0.72
Utilities	0.49
Health Care	0.47
Consumer Staples	0.31

Source: Thomson Reuters as of 12/31/08.

Table 3.2 S&P 500 Sector Returns

S&P 500 Sector	Total Return (12/31/2008–3/9/2009)
Information Technology	−13.6%
Health Care	−17.7%
Consumer Staples	−18.7%
Energy	−19.1%
Telecommunication Services	−20.1%
Materials	−20.4%
Utilities	−22.3%
Consumer Discretionary	−25.5%
Industrials	−35.2%
Financials	−50.0%

Source: Thomson Reuters, MSCI, Inc.[10]

Despite Technology's high beta, performance does not always follow this pattern. In investing, nothing is ever black and white. For example, the S&P 500 fell over 24 percent in the beginning of 2009, reaching a new low in March.[11] But, as shown in Table 3.2, Technology was the best-performing sector over this period, even surpassing traditionally "defensive" sectors like Health Care and Consumer Staples. What explains this? Likely, it had to do with features specific to this downturn—investors panicked over liquidity and stability in financial markets. Companies with high debt loads were punished on fears of potential default. It created a flight to safety where high-quality balance sheets were preferred. This worked to the Technology sector's advantage as it had, in aggregate, one of the lowest average debt loads in the market. Moreover, after the Tech bubble burst in 2000, many Technology firms significantly built up cash reserves. Investors viewed the sector as a safe haven and its traditionally economically sensitive nature was seemingly ignored.

However, in time, sentiment will change again, as it always does. Sometimes investors like earnings consistency, sometimes cash flow. The key is identifying the most important sentiment drivers at a given point in time and whether the Technology sector is positioned to benefit.

Professional Market Forecasts

Professional forecasts are a way to measure sentiment, and tracking them can provide insight as to what information is or isn't discounted into stock prices. Sentiment bell curves like the ones in Figure 3.10 provide good visual representations. These two histograms show annual market forecasts for the NASDAQ Composite in 2000 and 2001. The largest bars represent ranges with the highest number of forecasts—no bars represent ranges without forecasts.

During this time Technology was widely perceived as the hot sector. Indeed, people felt there was significant risk *not* investing in Tech. There were millions to be made, and everyone wanted a piece of the action—euphoria was widespread and it seemed the only direction the market could head was up. As seen in Figure 3.10, any sell-off like the one in 2000 was viewed as a simple correction—forecasts for 2001 were extremely bullish.

This, of course, proved false. Ebulliently bullish investors poured money into Technology and pushed valuations sky high. Euphoria blinded investors to the fact that myriad firms had unsustainable business

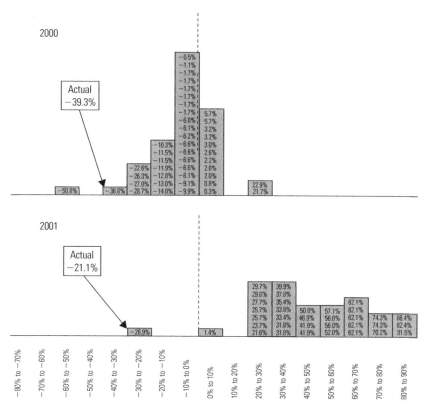

Figure 3.10   NASDAQ Annual Market Forecast Surveys
Source: BusinessWeek, Thomson Reuters, Fisher Investments.

models and weren't even profitable—nor likely to be. Eventually, the bubble burst and those still overweight in Technology suffered dramatic underperformance relative to the market. Massive euphoria about sectors, industries, or even the broad market is almost always a negative future indicator. Identifying such periods can be critical.

After the bubble burst, Technology led global indexes into a bear market. But it also led in the ensuing rebound—for a short period. This is fairly common with bear markets. Those sectors hit hardest in the later half of downturns often bounce the most in the early stages of the rebounds. However, the sector that led into the bear—in this case, Technology—may get an initial "dead-cat" bounce and seem like it will outperform the market in recovery. But, historically, those sectors tend to do poorly overall in the ensuing bull market. This is how Technology behaved. After a strong showing in 2003, the sector underperformed in 2004 and 2005. Typically, the biggest sector at the top that does the worst on the way down will drive a psychological over-hang. Too much fear about Technology still lingered because investors tend to want to "fight the last war" and avoid the sector that led the last bear market.

Chapter Recap

Like every other sector, Technology has a set of economic, political, and sentiment drivers. Identifying these drivers and how each influences performance relative to broader markets can help determine when to overweight and underweight the Technology sector.

- Economic growth is the single largest driver of the Technology sector.
- Other economic drivers helpful in predicting Technology performance include fixed investment, component shipments, inflation, share supply, and currency.
- Innovations and upgrade cycles are also capable of driving demand and performance of the Technology sector.
- Taxes, property rights, trade, and fiscal policy represent the largest political drivers of the sector.
- Sentiment has exerted a sizeable impact on the Technology sector's past performance. Examples include its perception as a "high beta" sector, widespread feelings of euphoria, and the mental overhang and risk aversion following the bursting of the Technology bubble.

II

NEXT STEPS: TECHNOLOGY DETAILS

TECHNOLOGY SECTOR BREAKDOWN

Now you've got the basics of how the Technology sector works, and an understanding of its history and some of its drivers. But a high-level understanding is just the beginning. Just like our overall economy, each sector is made of many distinct parts—some relatively similar to others and some quite unique. To better understand the whole, you must understand the parts.

Chapter 1 covered the major Technology products and services: semiconductors, computer hardware, communications equipment, consumer electronics, software, and services. These offerings come from a variety of firms with very different end markets and drivers. While an understanding of every company isn't necessary, a firm grasp on the major industries is vital before making any sector-related portfolio decisions. This chapter explores the sector's industries and how an investor can begin forming opinions on each.

GLOBAL INDUSTRY CLASSIFICATION STANDARD (GICS)

Before beginning, some definitions: The Global Industry Classification Standard (GICS) is a widely accepted framework for classifying companies into groups based on similarities. The GICS structure consists of 10 sectors, 24 industry groups, 68 industries, and 154 sub-industries. This structure offers four levels of hierarchy, ranging from the most general sector to the most specialized sub-industry:

- Sector
- Industry Group
- Industry
- Sub-Industry

Let's start by breaking down Technology into its different components. According to GICS, the Technology sector consists of 3 industry groups, 8 industries, and 16 sub-industries. Technology industries and corresponding sub-industries are:

Software

- Systems Software
- Application Software
- Home Entertainment Software

Computers & Peripherals

- Computer Hardware
- Computer Storage & Peripherals

Communications Equipment

- Communications Equipment

Semiconductors & Semiconductor Equipment

- Semiconductors
- Semiconductor Equipment

Electronic Equipment, Instruments & Components

- Electronic Components
- Electronic Equipment & Instruments
- Electronic Manufacturing Services
- Technology Distributors

IT Services

- Data Processing & Outsourced Services
- IT Consulting & Other Services

Internet Software & Services

- Internet Software & Services

Office Electronics

- Office Electronics

GLOBAL TECHNOLOGY BENCHMARKS

What's a benchmark? What does it do, and why is it necessary? A benchmark is your guide for building a stock portfolio. You can use any well-constructed index as a benchmark—examples are in Table 4.1. By studying a benchmark's (i.e., the index's) makeup, investors can assign expected risk and return to make underweight and overweight decisions for each industry. This is just as true for a sector as it is for the broader stock market, and there are many potential Technology sector benchmarks to choose from. (Benchmarks will be further explored with the top-down method in Chapter 7.)

Differences in Benchmarks

So what does the Technology investment universe look like? It depends on the benchmark, so choose carefully! The US Technology sector looks very different from Europe, Japan, and the Emerging Markets. Table 4.1 shows major domestic and international benchmark indexes and the percentage weight of each sector.

Sector weights show each sector's relative importance in driving overall index performance. While Technology is the smallest weight in the MSCI Europe, Australasia, Far East (EAFE) index, it's the largest weight in the S&P 500. Why does Technology have more relative weight in the US? One potential reason could be the US has historically had a freer economic environment with the necessary capital to cultivate new ideas and innovation. It's just tougher in many foreign

Table 4.1 Benchmark Differences

Sector	MSCI World	MSCI EAFE	S&P 500	Russell 2000	MSCI Emerging Markets
Consumer Discretionary	8.9%	9.6%	8.4%	11.0%	4.8%
Consumer Staples	11.1%	10.3%	12.9%	3.9%	5.8%
Energy	11.6%	8.5%	13.3%	4.4%	14.9%
Financials	18.6%	22.6%	13.3%	23.4%	22.8%
Health Care	11.9%	9.8%	14.8%	15.3%	2.9%
Industrials	10.9%	11.5%	11.1%	16.9%	7.7%
Information Technology	**10.2%**	**5.1%**	**15.3%**	**15.8%**	**10.8%**
Materials	5.8%	7.8%	2.9%	3.7%	12.8%
Telecommunication Services	5.3%	7.0%	3.8%	1.2%	13.6%
Utilities	5.7%	7.7%	4.2%	4.4%	4.0%
Total	100.0%	100.0%	100.0%	100.0%	100.0%

Source: Thomson Reuters; MSCI, Inc.[1] as of 12/31/08.

developed nations to start a new business than it is in the US. This led to the establishment of Silicon Valley and produced many of the industry behemoths still in existence today.

But sector and regional weights aren't fixed and can change over time due to performance differences, additions and deletions of firms to the indexes, and a variety of other factors. For example, Financials, though still a sizeable sector, lost tremendous relative weight in most indexes through the 2008 bear market. Tech used to be much larger in most indexes prior to the 2000 to 2003 bear market. And for many decades, Industrials dominated. Sectors are constantly in flux.

Understanding how your benchmark and the sectors in it are structured is crucial to developing a portfolio because wide weight deviations can exist across regions and benchmarks. For example, in some countries, Technology is by far the largest sector; in others, it's barely a few percent. Table 4.2 shows the Technology sector's weight in selected countries. (In this example, the MSCI All Country World

Table 4.2 Technology Weights by Country

Country	Technology Weight
Finland	54.3%
Korea	23.3%
US	15.5%
Sweden	14.1%
India	13.9%
Japan	12.3%
Germany	4.8%
Netherlands	4.0%
Canada	3.5%
China	2.9%
France	2.6%
Hong Kong	1.5%
Brazil	1.3%
Spain	0.6%
Australia	0.6%
Switzerland	0.4%
UK	0.3%

Source: Thomson Reuters; MSCI, Inc.[2] as of 12/31/08.

Index [ACWI] is used instead of the MSCI World to provide a wider scope.) Note: Tech in Finland more than *triples* the weight in the US. However, that weight is almost entirely concentrated in a single company: Nokia. Understanding how a sector is composed is vital— you don't want to think you're well diversified and find you're holding just one stock!

Industry Weights

Not only can sector weights vary, but so can industry weights— sometimes greatly, depending on the chosen benchmark. Table 4.3 shows the weight of each Technology industry within each benchmark.

Table 4.3 Technology Industry Weights

Industry	MSCI World	MSCI EAFE	S&P 500	Russell 2000	MSCI Emerging Markets
Software	22.8%	21.0%	23.9%	25.8%	2.2%
Computers & Peripherals	21.7%	8.4%	27.8%	5.2%	14.2%
Communications Equipment	17.6%	21.7%	16.4%	16.1%	1.1%
Semiconductors & Semiconductor Equipment	11.9%	7.6%	13.9%	17.2%	49.7%
IT Services	9.0%	5.7%	6.4%	11.6%	10.0%
Internet Software & Services	6.9%	1.8%	9.3%	12.5%	5.6%
Electronic Equipment & Instruments	6.8%	21.6%	1.7%	11.6%	17.3%
Office Electronics	3.2%	12.2%	0.6%	0.0%	0.0%
Total	100.0%	100.0%	100.0%	100.0%	100.0%

Source: Thomson Reuters; MSCI, Inc.[3] as of 12/31/08.

Understanding these weights allows you to not only properly weight your portfolio relative to your benchmark, but also effectively use your time by focusing on the most important components. For Technology, the largest industries are Software, Computers & Peripherals, Communications Equipment, and Semiconductor & Semiconductor Equipment—making up the majority of the weight in most benchmarks, and therefore the focus of much of this book.

A Concentrated Group

Another distinguishing Technology characteristic is the industries are concentrated in relatively few, very large players. Table 4.4 shows the percentage weight of the 10 largest firms in each industry (using the MSCI World). With concentrations ranging from 68 to 100 percent of the industry, the largest firms truly dominate.

Table 4.4 Concentration of Technology Industries

Industry	Concentration of 10 Largest Firms
Communications Equipment	99.2%
Computers & Peripherals	95.0%
Electronic Equipment, Instruments & Components	68.0%
Internet Software & Services	100.0%*
IT Services	73.5%
Office Electronics	100.0%*
Semiconductors & Semiconductor Equipment	76.2%
Software	88.0%

Source: Thomson Reuters; MSCI, Inc.[4] as of 12/31/08.
*Less than 10 companies in respective industry.

TECHNOLOGY INDUSTRY BREAKDOWN

Now that you know the general sector breakdown, we can examine Technology's larger industries (based on their weight in the MSCI World Index) in greater detail. They break down into the following industries and sub-industries:

- Software
- Computers & Peripherals
- Communications Equipment
- Semiconductors & Semiconductor Equipment

Software

First, we'll start with Software: The Software industry develops, markets, distributes, and supports virtually all forms of software. The industry is segmented further into three sub-industries:

- Systems Software
- Application Software
- Home Entertainment Software

Table 4.5 lists the 10 largest Software firms globally. It's easy to see the heavy concentration in the US.

Table 4.5 10 Largest Global Software Companies

Company	Sub-industry	Country	Market Cap	% of Total Industry Market Cap
Microsoft	Systems Software	US	$172,930	36.7%
Oracle	Systems Software	US	$89,469	19.0%
Nintendo	Home Entertainment Software	Japan	$52,745	11.2%
SAP	Application Software	Germany	$43,007	9.1%
Activision Blizzard	Home Entertainment Software	US	$11,443	2.4%
Symantec	Systems Software	US	$11,345	2.4%
Adobe Systems	Application Software	US	$11,304	2.4%
CA	Systems Software	US	$9,604	2.0%
Intuit	Application Software	US	$7,614	1.6%
Oracle Japan	Systems Software	Japan	$5,426	1.2%

Source: Thomson Reuters; MSCI, Inc.[5] as of 12/31/08.

Systems Software   Systems Software is the largest of the group. Firms in this sub-industry construct programs that run and help manage hardware. Since almost all forms of hardware require software to function, products in this market are less discretionary in nature. Here, you'll find operating systems, middleware, virtualization (explained further in Chapter 6), and security software. Industry giants Microsoft and Oracle sit at the top of this market.

Application Software   Application Software is a very diverse sub-industry. Firms in this sub-industry design software to perform specific "applications," or tasks. The possibilities are near limitless and depend only on the ability to imagine new tasks to perform. As such, firms included in this sub-industry produce software for human resources, graphic design, customer relationship management (CRM), and tax planning, to name a very few.

SAP and Adobe Systems are the largest pure Software players in this group. But many software firms compete in multiple markets and don't fall into the Application Software sub-industry—Oracle is a prime example. While it's classified as Systems Software, it happens to be SAP's largest and most formidable competitor in application software. Certain programs from Microsoft also compete in this category, like its Office Suite. Put another way, the application software market is much larger than the MSCI World Index sub-industry suggests.

A Hungry Giant

Competing with SAP was no small task for Oracle. Since Oracle's purchase of PeopleSoft in 2005, the firm has completed or engaged in over 50 acquisitions. This impressive string of purchases expanded Oracle's application software portfolio and improved competitiveness with its German rival. This also created extensive cross-selling opportunities, which the firm has used to maintain growth.

Home Entertainment Software   The Home Entertainment Software sub-industry is much smaller than its peers. This is true of both size (aggregate market capitalization) and the number of firms. It's also less diverse because of its focus on a single area: video games. Within this sub-industry, Nintendo, Activision-Blizzard, and Electronic Arts are the largest players. While Nintendo is exclusive to its proprietary video game systems, most firms in this market produce games for a variety of platforms. These include different video game consoles, handheld systems, cell phones, personal computers, and the Internet. While not categorized as such, Microsoft and Sony are also significant players in this market.

Software Operations   Producing software doesn't require massive manufacturing facilities or huge supplies of raw materials—it's simply code. As such, one of the highest input costs is research and development. Firms are constantly investing in the development of new programs and upgrading existing ones.

The relatively low capital intensity means initial barriers to entry are fairly low. All you need is an idea and someone capable of writing code. However, distributing and marketing the software is a much harder task. The software market actually encompasses hundreds, if not thousands, of small, non-publicly traded firms. Some go public, but most often, if there's a promising idea from a small upstart firm, it's acquired by a larger publicly traded firm. The idea is then developed, marketed, and distributed through a larger network and customer base.

Licensing New Growth

One of the most-watched metrics in software is *new license growth*. When a software firm sells its product to a new customer or sells a new product to an existing customer, that's a new license. It's one of the better indicators of "true" demand and provides insight into future sales.

For example, in order to receive product enhancements, upgrades, and support, many customers must pay for maintenance contracts. These contracts vary in length but provide software firms recurring and stable revenue streams. A higher number of new software licenses typically translates into higher future maintenance and support revenue.

Product distribution is done in a few different ways. Most consumer-related software is downloaded online or purchased in packages from retailers, but the enterprise market is different. In the traditional model, customers buy software through upfront licensing fees, then pay ongoing fees for maintenance and support. Installation is typically done by the customer.

However, new disruptive models have begun to emerge, like Software-as-a-Service (SaaS). Also referred to as "on-demand" software and often delivered over the Internet, this allows customers to purchase programs based on the number of end users or usage. This can reduce installation time and provide easier access to product support.

Drivers   Software demand is tied closely to the demand drivers for hardware sales, particularly computers, because a significant percentage of hardware comes pre-bundled with software. In computers, this is most often the operating system, but it can include antivirus programs, Internet browsers, word processors, etc.

Upgrade cycles also play a major role in the software industry, particularly operating system upgrades. Consumers and businesses often upgrade to newer versions to take advantage of the enhanced features, which in turn drives demand for other programs that function with the new operating system.

Hand in hand with upgrade cycles, product support (or the lack thereof) can also drive demand. As firms release new products, the cost of supporting older versions becomes increasingly uneconomical. Eventually, software vendors often cease support for outdated versions. The businesses still running older programs are then forced to upgrade to ensure ongoing support.

Earnings Drivers While the aforementioned factors drive sales, there are additional factors driving earnings. Product mix is one of the most important. Like many areas of the sector, the software industry is deflationary—older products typically have lower price tags. This makes upgrade cycles all the more important in driving earnings. When new products are released they often sell for premium prices and have higher margins. Successful adoption bodes well for the software vendor's earnings. Distribution methods also have an impact. The push to distribute software online, for example, can lead to greater efficiencies and lower costs relative to physical production.

Computers & Peripherals

Firms that design, develop, and sell computers and related parts fall into the Computers & Peripherals industry. It's segmented further into two sub-industries:

- Computer Hardware
- Computer Storage & Peripherals

Table 4.6 shows the 10 largest Computers & Peripherals firms globally. This list includes some computer heavyweights most investors are likely familiar with.

Computer Hardware Computer Hardware is the larger of the two sub-industries. Mostly original equipment manufacturers (OEMs), these firms produce computer products like servers and workstations. This is where you'll find branded PC manufacturers, like HP, Apple, and Dell. It's heavily concentrated in the US, with a respectable showing from Japan.

Computer Storage & Peripherals Firms in the Computer Storage & Peripherals sub-industry manufacture storage devices or peripherals, with most market cap weight in storage. EMC, NetApp, and Western Digital are dominant players in the storage market. EMC and NetApp

Table 4.6 10 Largest Global Computers & Peripherals Companies

Company	Sub-industry	Country	Market Cap	% of Total Industry Market Cap
IBM	Computer Hardware	US	$113,065	30.2%
Hewlett-Packard	Computer Hardware	US	$87,684	23.5%
Apple	Computer Hardware	US	$75,871	20.3%
EMC	Computer Storage & Peripherals	US	$21,367	5.7%
Dell	Computer Hardware	US	$19,911	5.3%
Toshiba	Computer Hardware	Japan	$13,072	3.5%
Fujitsu	Computer Hardware	Japan	$9,796	2.6%
NEC	Computer Hardware	Japan	$6,650	1.8%
NetApp	Computer Storage & Peripherals	US	$4,612	1.2%
Seiko Epson	Computer Storage & Peripherals	Japan	$3,041	0.8%

Source: Thomson Reuters, MSCI, Inc.[6] as of 12/31/08.

are competitors, producing enterprise-level storage devices. Western Digital, though in the same market, doesn't compete directly with EMC and NetApp. Western Digital produces hard disk drives used *within* enterprise-level storage devices, but they're also used in PCs, consumer electronics, DVRs, etc.

Peripherals firms produce a variety of products (like computer mice, printers, monitors, etc.), but all for the same end market—computers.

Computers & Peripherals Operations Most hardware manufacturers operate similarly, with a few exceptions. All sell hardware products, but not every firm produces the components within. These are often sourced from third-party manufacturers and used to build final products. For PC manufacturers, this is true for virtually every component. The microprocessor, motherboard, memory, hard disk drive (HDD), and liquid crystal display (LCD) are all sourced from third parties. Each component is usually highly interchangeable with little differentiation in product functionality among brands.

Manufacturing in this industry varies. Some firms assemble their products wholly in-house. But many firms outsource a portion of manufacturing to third parties. Outsourced manufacturers, located primarily in Southeast Asia, build final products based on the OEM's design specifications. Both models have advantages and disadvantages. By outsourcing production, firms can reduce manufacturing costs—particularly helpful during periods of weak demand. However, keeping manufacturing in-house increases control over quality and production volumes.

Many products can also be customized with specific hardware and software during the assembly process. Firms doing this "customization" are known as value-added resellers (VARs).

Once assembled, hardware is sold through a few different channels: direct, distributors, and retail. Dell is well known for its *direct* model—selling directly to customers with no "middle man"—although the firm has recently pushed into retail. The enterprise market commonly uses both a direct sales force (for more complex and high-end products like mainframes and workstations) and *distributors*—one-stop shops for myriad technology-related products. The *retail* channel, stores like Best Buy or Office Max, is mostly for consumers.

Drivers   The Computers & Peripherals industry is particularly economically sensitive. Businesses and consumers are simply less likely to make large ticket purchases when the economy's weak (as demonstrated in Figure 3.4), and sales rebound during periods of more robust growth. Emerging markets growth has become a particularly important driver. Businesses and consumers from these regions represent an increasingly large portion of global computer sales growth.

Just like software, upgrade cycles can be a significant driver. For example, new versions of Microsoft's Windows have typically led to increasing PC purchases, as do new generations of microprocessors. The combination of software- and hardware-driven upgrade cycles is sometimes referred to as "Wintel"—a combination of Windows and Intel. Structural changes can also spur upgrade cycles, like the transition from floppy disks to CD-ROM.

Demand for Internet access is another significant driver—particularly in emerging markets where penetration is still low. Many people own PCs solely for accessing the Internet, and devices such as netbooks have grown in popularity in emerging and developed markets alike.

A driver more related to storage than computers is the need for increasing amounts of digital data. More enterprises and consumers do business online, not to mention dramatic increases in video and multimedia content. Larger and more robust storage devices are required for storing all that rich data.

Earnings Drivers   An important item to note: Top-line growth does not always translate into bottom-line growth. Sales and earnings can have disparate drivers. Earnings can be influenced by multiple factors—input prices (parts and labor) being one of the largest. PCs are built of the same basic components—many highly commoditized. So if there's global oversupply of LCD panels or memory, prices are likely to fall. This reduces the total cost of manufacturing a PC and can expand profit margins. And it can work the other way, too! If supply of certain components falls, prices rise and so do manufacturing costs. This shrinks profit margins.

As for labor, it's generally more expensive in developed markets than in emerging markets. Having a larger percentage of manufacturing in low-cost regions can help drive earnings, which is why many hardware manufacturers have shifted production to Southeast Asia.

Communications Equipment

Communications Equipment firms design, develop, and market communications equipment globally. This industry has just one sub-industry, also titled Communications Equipment. Table 4.7 lists the 10 largest Communications Equipment firms globally.

Communications Equipment   Though the Communications Equipment industry and sub-industry are one and the same, they can be segmented into different categories—products manufactured for either the fixed-line or wireless market. Firms that focus mostly on fixed line, like industry giant Cisco Systems, produce equipment for networking and accessing the Internet (e.g., routers, switches, fiber optics).

The wireless market consists of two types of firms: infrastructure manufacturers and mobile handset manufacturers. While some do both, firms leveraged to the infrastructure market produce base transceiver stations and antennae that enable GSM and CDMA networks to function. Handset producers manufacture cell phones based on these same technologies. Nokia, Research in Motion, and Ericsson are leaders in different areas of the wireless market, which is largely dominated by non-US firms. However, many top mobile handset manufacturers are classified in other industries. For example, Samsung is a major handset producer, but is considered a Semiconductor firm, while Apple is classified under Computer Hardware. And some major handset producers, like LG Electronics, are in entirely different sectors.

Table 4.7 10 Largest Global Communications Equipment Companies

Company	Sub-industry	Country	Market Cap	% of Total Industry Market Cap
Cisco Systems	Communications Equipment	US	$95,438	31.3%
Qualcomm	Communications Equipment	US	$59,316	19.5%
Nokia	Communications Equipment	Finland	$58,649	19.2%
Research in Motion	Communications Equipment	Canada	$22,695	7.4%
Ericsson	Communications Equipment	Sweden	$22,192	7.3%
Corning Inc.	Communications Equipment	US	$14,813	4.9%
Motorola	Communications Equipment	US	$10,040	3.3%
Juniper Networks	Communications Equipment	US	$9,244	3.0%
Harris	Communications Equipment	US	$5,121	1.7%
Alcatel-Lucent	Communications Equipment	France	$4,939	1.6%

Source: Thomson Reuters; MSCI, Inc.[7] as of 12/31/08.

Communications Equipment Operations   From a manufacturing perspective, most Communications Equipment firms operate similarly to Computers & Peripherals firms. Companies outsource some or all of manufacturing and use third party component suppliers.

Distribution is similar to Computers & Peripherals as well. The enterprise market purchases equipment directly from suppliers or through third party distributors, and consumers use retail outlets. However, there are significant differences. In the PC supply chain, retail outlets are actual stores like Best Buy and Wal-Mart with broad product lines. But consumers buying handsets usually buy from retail stores owned by the service providers (like AT&T, Verizon, T-Mobile, etc.). These service providers typically subsidize mobile phone costs to attract new subscribers.

Also unique is mobile handset manufacturers can designate certain telecommunications firms as exclusive phone providers. For example, at the time of this writing, Apple iPhone users in the US can only get phone services through AT&T.

Drivers Drivers vary depending on the product, but like most Technology industries, economic growth is critically important. Upgrade cycles play a role as well. This is most obvious in the wireless space where every generation of network technology requires new investment in equipment. Much of the developed world has migrated to third generation (3G) networks, and the transition to 4G is already underway. Hence, increasing capital expenditures by telecom carriers can significantly influence growth.

Volumes and types of digital data carried over networks can also drive demand for infrastructure equipment. Fixed-line and wireless networks both have a finite amount of bandwidth—they become increasingly loaded as more users are added or more data are transferred. Demand is also rising for multimedia functionality and high-bandwidth content like video. To avoid congestion, network operators may add additional infrastructure or upgrade existing equipment.

When it comes to mobile handset demand, emerging markets are major contributors. The majority of unit phone purchases come from these regions where economic growth and rising incomes have placed wireless service within reach of consumers. This trend is likely to continue given these regions' low wireless penetration levels. In other words, relative to developed markets, there are fewer wireless subscribers as a percentage of the total population, which leaves more room for growth.

In developed markets, new subscribers are less of a growth driver because some developed markets have penetration levels above 100 percent—on average, each wireless customer has more than one phone. In these regions, growth is mostly driven by handset replacements and upgrades. Because of greater levels of wealth, demand for high-end handsets is concentrated in these regions.

Earnings Drivers   As for earnings drivers, intense and growing competition puts downward pressure on earnings—for both infrastructure equipment and mobile handsets. In fact, the bidding process in wireless infrastructure is so competitive that supplying equipment for new network rollouts is often a drag on margins. Suppliers take an upfront hit in order to gain more profitable service and maintenance business down the road. This makes economies of scale critical—a favorable attribute for infrastructure and handset manufacturers alike.

Semiconductors & Semiconductor Equipment

Semiconductors & Semiconductor Equipment firms design, develop, and market both semiconductors and related production equipment. It's segmented into two sub-industries:

- Semiconductors
- Semiconductor Equipment

Table 4.8 shows the 10 largest Semiconductors & Semiconductor Equipment firms globally. Here, the largest player, Intel, simply swamps the other firms and is four times larger than its next-largest competitor.

Semiconductors   Semiconductors is the larger of the two sub-industries.[8] These firms manufacture integrated circuits for myriad purposes and end markets—microprocessors, memory, power amplifiers, converters, and many other forms. US firms make up over half of the Semiconductor weight (in the MSCI World Index), followed by Japan and the Netherlands. There is also a heavy concentration in Emerging Markets, particularly Korea and Taiwan.

Semiconductor Equipment   Semiconductor Equipment is a much smaller sub-industry.[10] There are fewer firms and the aggregate market

Table 4.8 10 Largest Global Semiconductors & Semiconductor Equipment Companies

Company	Sub-industry	Country	Market Cap	% of Total Industry Market Cap
Intel	Semiconductors	US	$81,539	39.2%
Texas Instruments	Semiconductors	US	$20,121	9.7%
Applied Materials	Semiconductor Equipment	US	$13,461	6.5%
ASML Holding	Semiconductor Equipment	Netherlands	$7,644	3.7%
Broadcom	Semiconductors	US	$7,231	3.5%
Tokyo Electron	Semiconductor Equipment	Japan	$6,176	3.0%
STMicroelectronics	Semiconductors	France	$6,049	2.9%
ROHM	Semiconductors	Japan	$5,675	2.7%
Analog Devices	Semiconductors	US	$5,538	2.7%
Altera	Semiconductors	US	$4,969	2.4%

Source: Thomson Reuters; MSCI, Inc.[9] as of 12/31/08.

cap and size of the total market is smaller. These firms manufacture specialized equipment used in the semiconductor production process—chip manufacturers are their primary customers. Mostly concentrated in the US, the industry leader is Applied Materials.

Semiconductors & Semiconductor Equipment Operations   Producing chips on a large scale is highly capital intensive. Not only is research and development a significant input cost, but firms also need massive fabrication plants and expensive production equipment. This generally makes property, plant, and equipment (PP&E) one of the largest assets on a chip producer's balance sheet. It also means firms incur heavy depreciation expenses.

Semiconductor producers operate under multiple business models. There's the traditional, vertically integrated model, as well as *fabless* and *fab-lite*. Vertically integrated semiconductor firms, also known as integrated device manufacturers (IDMs), own and operate all of the fabrication plants producing their chips. They're responsible for building new facilities and maintaining and upgrading existing ones. This is the most capital intensive out of the three models, but it also provides the greatest control over quality and output.

In a completely *fabless* model, semiconductor firms outsource all manufacturing to third parties, referred to as *foundries*. This frees capital to be used in other areas, like research and development. It also relieves the burden of constantly upgrading to new technology and eliminates the impact of low utilization in periods of sluggish demand. However, it reduces control over quality and output, meaning fabless firms could potentially be unable to meet demand. This is why some companies have employed *fab-lite* models—a cross between the two where only a portion of manufacturing is outsourced to foundries.

Business models of semiconductor equipment firms don't differ much from those of machine manufacturers from other sectors and industries. Typically, these firms produce equipment subject to customer evaluation and testing cycles before release. However, due to the highly specialized nature of semiconductor equipment, testing cycles are longer. Because semiconductors are produced on an exceptionally small scale, precision and accuracy are of the utmost importance.

Sales and distribution are relatively straightforward. Equipment manufacturers primarily market and distribute products directly to chip producers. This includes IDMs, foundries, and firms performing testing and assembly services. However, semiconductor firms (mostly IDMs) ship products to customers in various stages of the hardware manufacturing chain. This includes third party distributors, contract manufacturers, foundries, and even original design manufacturers. There is minimal use of the retail market.

A variety of metrics are used to track company performance and industry fundamentals. One of the most common is the book-to-bill ratio (see Chapter 2). Capacity utilization is also tracked. This represents the percentage of total potential output currently in production. This information is reported quarterly for global chip manufacturers by the Semiconductor Industry Association (www.sia-online.org). This organization also issues monthly data on global sales of semiconductors.

Drivers   Semiconductors are used in most modern electronics, with computers and mobile handsets representing almost two-thirds of consumption. Strong sales of PCs and mobile phones generally lead to higher unit shipments of semiconductors. And because these industries are economically sensitive, semiconductor demand is also greatly influenced by economic growth.

Demand for semiconductor equipment is largely dependent on semiconductor firms building new fabrication plants. These facilities require significant capital expenditures and are most likely to be built when economic conditions and demand for chips are strong. In fact, this industry is highly cyclical and one of the more economically sensitive in the Technology sector. Investment in new chip technologies and equipment often follows recessions and periods of prolonged underinvestment.

New generations of manufacturing technology can be important drivers for Semiconductor Equipment. For example, much of the industry has transitioned, or is in the process of doing so, to 300mm silicon wafers from the previous 200mm standard—requiring new specialized equipment compatible with the larger size. Feature sizes on chips are also getting smaller, which makes manufacturers invest in new equipment that can produce at smaller scales.

Earnings Drivers   Like other areas of Technology, semiconductor prices suffer from deflation, which can negatively impact earnings. Newer, more advanced chips typically have higher price tags and margins than older versions—but this advantage is fleeting. Pretty quickly, the next version comes and pushes down prices on the previous generation, so manufacturers must constantly innovate to maintain earnings. This is particularly true for digital chips, which have become increasingly commoditized relative to analog on stiffer competition.

They must be smaller, faster, and more efficient than previous generations to fetch a higher price.

Capacity utilization can also impact earnings. During periods of strong demand, manufacturers operate at much higher utilization rates. This reduces fixed costs as a percent of total output and helps drive margin expansion. Other factors influencing earnings include manufacturing models (e.g., fabless and/or fab-lite models described earlier), economies of scale, and improved productivity, to name a few.

Electronic Equipment, Instruments & Components

Many firms that cannot be classified into other industries fall into Electronic Equipment, Instruments & Components, which is a bit of a grab bag of sub-industries. These firms design, develop, market, and distribute myriad forms of electronic equipment and components. Its four sub-industries include:

- Electronic Components
- Electronic Equipment & Instruments
- Electronic Manufacturing Services
- Technology Distributors

Table 4.9 shows the 10 largest Electronic Equipment, Instruments & Components firms globally. Here, there is heavy concentration in Japan rather than in the US.

Electronic Components Electronic Components is the largest sub-industry by aggregate market capitalization and total number of firms.[11] Japan is again home to most firms in this market. These firms manufacture products like semiconductor photomasks, semiconductor packaging materials, chip capacitors, and LCD panels. The key commonality is all products are "components" built into devices higher up in the supply chain. Although mostly known for its cell phones, Kyocera is this sub-industry's leader.[13]

Table 4.9 10 Largest Global Electronic Equipment, Instruments & Components Companies

Company	Sub-industry	Country	Market Cap	% of Total Industry Market Cap
Kyocera	Electronic Components	Japan	$13,464	10.6%
Hitachi	Electronic Equipment & Instruments	Japan	$12,819	10.1%
Fujifilm	Electronic Equipment & Instruments	Japan	$11,070	8.7%
Keyence	Electronic Equipment & Instruments	Japan	$10,089	7.9%
Murata Manufacturing	Electronic Components	Japan	$8,697	6.8%
Tyco Electronics	Electronic Manufacturing Services	US	$7,418	5.8%
Hoya	Electronic Components	Japan	$7,395	5.8%
Agilent Technologies	Electronic Equipment & Instruments	US	$5,501	4.3%
Nidec	Electronic Components	Japan	$5,489	4.3%
TDK	Electronic Components	Japan	$4,646	3.6%

Source: Thomson Reuters; MSCI, Inc.[12] as of 12/31/08.

Electronic Equipment & Instruments Electronic Equipment & Instruments is the second largest sub-industry by market capitalization.[14] Mostly concentrated in Japan, these firms manufacture electronic products for a variety of end markets. Hitachi is the largest of the group and a good example of the diversity of product lines. The firm manufactures hard disk drives, servers, LCD panels, semiconductors, nuclear power plants, elevators, circuit boards, and televisions, to name a few. It's truly a technology conglomerate. Such diversity of products and end markets is not uncommon among Japanese Technology firms.

Electronic Manufacturing Services The third largest sub-industry is Electronic Manufacturing Services,[15] which is a more cohesive sub-industry than the previous two. These firms are all contract manufacturers enlisted primarily by Technology firms to build final end products. Tyco Electronics is this sub-industry's largest firm within the MSCI world. But if you include Emerging Markets, Taiwan's Hon Hai Precision Industry is the dominant global player. The firm produces PCs, mobile handsets, and various electronic devices for virtually all major Technology OEMs.

Technology Distributors   Technology Distributors is the smallest sub-industry in the entire Technology sector by market capitalization.[16] These firms act as middlemen in the technology supply chain, aggregating stockpiles of components, equipment, and systems that are resold to enterprise customers and retailers.

Operations and Drivers   Because Electronic Equipment, Instruments & Components is a diverse, grab-bag industry, operations and drivers vary even within sub-industries and individual firms. Some Electronic Equipment & Instruments firms operate similarly to hardware manufacturers, while many are more similar to Industrials firms. For example, a significant portion of Hitachi's business is derived from power plants and industrial equipment like elevators, so growth is typically more dependent on physical infrastructure spending. However, its servers, LCD panels, and semiconductors are leveraged to IT spending—making it difficult to nail down any firm-wide drivers. Typically, discrete business lines will have unique drivers.

Electronic Manufacturing Services firms operate in several different ways. Some are contracted purely for manufacturing services—the product design is done by the OEM or contracting firm. Margins for these services are thin, so manufacturers try to take on as much volume as possible. Certain firms, however, operate with a more specialized business model, taking on smaller but more complex and higher margin projects. To try to improve profitability further, some firms also offer product design services. Drivers in this sub-industry also vary because firms are contracted by many different end markets, some outside of the Technology sector.

IT Services

There are many types of IT services, but this industry includes firms offering non-manufacturing related services. The two sub-industries are:

- Data Processing & Outsourced Services
- IT Consulting & Other Services

Table 4.10 is a list of the 10 largest IT Services firms globally. Folks may presume some of these firms—like Visa, Mastercard, Paychex, and

Table 4.10 Ten Largest Global IT Services Companies

Company	Sub-industry	Country	Market Cap	% of Total Industry Market Cap
Visa	Data Processing & Outsourced Services	US	$23,549	13.8%
Automatic Data Processing	Data Processing & Outsourced Services	US	$19,980	11.7%
Accenture	IT Consulting & Other Services	US	$19,915	11.7%
MasterCard	Data Processing & Outsourced Services	US	$14,062	8.3%
NTT Data	IT Consulting & Other Services	Japan	$11,078	6.5%
Western Union	Data Processing & Outsourced Services	US	$10,456	6.1%
Paychex	Data Processing & Outsourced Services	US	$9,482	5.6%
Fiserv	Data Processing & Outsourced Services	US	$5,825	3.4%
Capgemini	IT Consulting & Other Services	France	$5,574	3.3%
Computer Sciences Corporation	Data Processing & Outsourced Services	US	$5,323	3.1%

Source: Thomson Reuters; MSCI, Inc.[17] as of 12/31/08.

Western Union—are Financials firms, but, based on their services and product offering, they belong in the Technology sector.

Data Processing & Outsourced Services Data Processing & Outsourced Services is the larger of the two sub-industries.[18] Most firms in this market process credit card transactions, payroll, money transfers, or other forms of data. Some firms offer services such as systems integration and business process outsourcing. Visa, Automatic Data Processing, and MasterCard are the largest players by market capitalization. This sub-industry is almost entirely concentrated in the US.

IT Consulting & Other Services IT Consulting & Other Services firms offer consulting, systems integration, and business process outsourcing. Outsourcing can include human resources services, network operations, or data center management. Accenture is this sub-industry's largest player, but this is another sub-industry with a heavy concentration in Emerging Markets—in this case India. And though IBM isn't classified in this sub-industry, it is the world's largest provider of IT services.

Operations and Drivers IT Services firms have two goals: expand geographically and reduce costs. Fierce competition gives those with cheaper and more widely available services an advantage. And keep in mind, these firms compete against larger and better-funded players in the hardware and software markets (like IBM). Because labor is one of the largest input costs, a larger percentage of workers in low-cost regions can improve margins. India has been a popular choice given its well-educated, English-speaking population.

The data-processing side of this industry is affected by diverse factors, depending on the end market. A sizeable portion of the market is leveraged to financial transactions, so increasing consumer and enterprise spending drives growth. Those involved in payroll processing, however, are driven by employment levels.

Internet Software & Services

Internet Software & Services has one sub-industry of the same title. These firms use some form of online technology platform to generate revenue. This differs from online retailers, like Amazon, that use the Internet as a primary sales channel but also have physical infrastructure and inventory. Led by industry giant Google, Internet search is the dominant service offered. Google also represents over half of the industry's weight. Table 4.11 lists the seven dominant global players (the MSCI World Internet Software & Services Industry only consists of seven firms).

Operations and Drivers Most Internet search firms have two similar business lines—search and display (banner ads). Both are leveraged to advertising spending. In general, advertising budgets increase during periods of strong economic growth and are one of the first areas to be cut in periods of weak or declining growth. The number of aggregate Internet subscribers also plays a role, as does the quality of search results—the more relevant sponsored links are to the actual search term, the more likely a user will click through.

Table 4.11 Seven Largest Global Internet Software & Services Companies

Company	Sub-industry	Country	Market Cap	% of Total Industry Market Cap
Google	Internet Software & Services	US	$73,693	52.4%
Yahoo! Japan	Internet Software & Services	Japan	$23,873	17.0%
eBay	Internet Software & Services	US	$17,826	12.7%
Yahoo!	Internet Software & Services	US	$16,907	12.0%
VeriSign	Internet Software & Services	US	$3,702	2.6%
Akamai Technologies	Internet Software & Services	US	$2,552	1.8%
United Internet	Internet Software & Services	Germany	$2,198	1.6%

Source: Thomson Reuters; MSCI, Inc.[19] as of 12/31/08.

Table 4.12 Six Largest Global Office Electronics Companies

Company	Sub-industry	Country	Market Cap	% of Total Industry Market Cap
Canon	Office Electronics	Japan	$40,756	62.4%
Ricoh	Office Electronics	Japan	$9,236	14.1%
Xerox	Office Electronics	US	$6,899	10.6%
Konica Minolta	Office Electronics	Japan	$4,000	6.1%
Neopost	Office Electronics	France	$2,801	4.3%
Brother Industries	Office Electronics	Japan	$1,613	2.5%

Source: Thomson Reuters; MSCI, Inc.[20] 12/31/08.

Banner ads are less targeted than search, making them more sensitive to weak economic conditions and budget cutbacks.

Office Electronics

Office Electronics is Technology's smallest industry by aggregate market capitalization and number of firms.[21] Heavily concentrated in Japan, these firms produce electronic office equipment like copiers and printers. Canon is by far the largest player at over 60 percent of the industry's weight. Also, many computer hardware manufacturers compete in this market, though they're not classified in this industry. Table 4.12 lists the six largest global Office Electronics firms (the MSCI World Office Electronics Industry only consists of six firms).

Operations and Drivers   These firms sell office equipment to businesses and consumers, though the top two players, Canon and Ricoh, have significant exposure to digital cameras—a market almost entirely driven by consumer spending. Operations are similar to other hardware and equipment manufacturers with one notable difference: Following the sale of a copier or printer, these firms generate recurring revenue through sales of highly profitable supplies (e.g., ink and toner). Demand for this equipment has largely been driven by generational transitions like from print-only to multi-function devices, and from black and white to color.

Chapter Recap

The Technology sector is comprised of a variety of industries, including Software; Computers & Peripherals; Communications Equipment; Semiconductors & Semiconductor Equipment; Electronic Equipment, Instruments & Components; IT Services; Internet Software & Services; and Office Electronics. While most of these industries are economically sensitive, each possesses unique operating environments and drivers.

- The Software industry includes producers of system, application, and home entertainment software. Most firms generate sales from upfront licensing fees and charge customers for ongoing support and maintenance. Hardware demand and upgrade cycles are two of the primary drivers.
- The Computers & Peripherals industry includes hardware, storage, and peripheral manufacturers. Many companies in this market source components from third party manufacturers, which are built into final products. Drivers include strong economic growth, upgrade cycles, Internet penetration, and increasing digital data.
- Companies in the Communications Equipment industry produce equipment for fixed-line and wireless networks, as well as mobile handsets. Upgrade cycles, demand for multimedia content, and demographics are all drivers.
- Semiconductors & Semiconductor Equipment companies manufacture chips and related production equipment. Operations are carried out through vertically integrated, fab-lite, and fabless business models. Drivers include PC and mobile handset demand, innovation, new production technology, and economic growth.
- Electronic Equipment, Instruments & Components companies offer a wide range of products and services. As such, operations and drivers vary depending on the sub-industry, end markets, and company in question.
- Companies in the IT Services industry provide data processing, consulting, systems integration, and business process outsourcing. Global scale and offshore operations are important attributes.
- Internet Software & Services is leveraged to the Internet search market, with advertising spending as the single largest driver.
- Office Electronics is a small industry with majority of the weight concentrated in one company. These firms sell upfront equipment and generate recurring revenue from supplies.

5

CHALLENGES IN THE INFORMATION TECHNOLOGY SECTOR

When analyzing a sector, identifying opportunities is just half the battle. Smart analysis should also root out potential challenges and the risks those challenges pose to near and longer-term growth of the sector, and the individual industries and firms therein. Some challenges are universal to all sectors—like competition, higher taxes, integrating acquisitions, etc. Here, we will focus on three of the more significant challenges specific to Tech: product maturity and obsolescence, extreme fluctuations in supply and demand, and threats to intellectual property. Understanding the risk these challenges may present can help you make better investment decisions.

PRODUCT MATURITY AND OBSOLESCENCE

The Technology sector is typically characterized by fast-paced, constant innovation. But most "hot" new markets eventually face maturity and obsolescence. A groundbreaking product hits the market and experiences rapid growth. Witnessing its success, new entrants appear, wanting to get in on the action, developing variations of the product or new generations. Over time, the market becomes crowded and eventually saturated. Weaker players are then typically forced out or acquired.

This is evident with growth of computer sales. Proliferation of the Internet in the 1990s fueled rapid growth in computer hardware demand (not just PCs, but also servers and other infrastructure), but over time, the market became increasingly saturated. Figure 5.1 shows slowing growth of worldwide PC shipments over the last five years, even as total unit volumes rose (Note: PCs include desktops, notebooks, ultra portables, and x86 servers but do not include handhelds). Strong demand for notebooks and portable PCs has kept overall growth from slowing more sharply. But the server and desktop market is much more mature—shipments grew just 5.1 percent in 2007 and fell 5.2 percent in 2008.[1]

Maturing, competitive markets tend to result in increased acquisitions and consolidation. The first decade of the twenty-first century

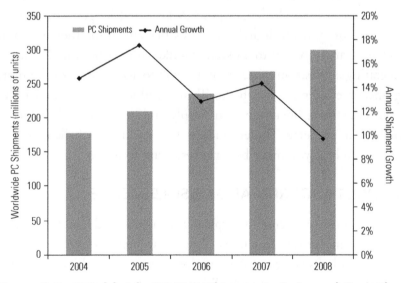

Figure 5.1   Worldwide PC Unit Shipments & Annual Growth
Source: IDC Worldwide Quarterly PC Tracker.

was no different for PC manufacturers. Some of the notable acquisitions in recent years are:

- In 2002, Hewlett-Packard purchased Compaq.
- In 2004, Gateway purchased eMachines.
- In 2005, Lenovo purchased IBM's PC division.
- In 2007, Acer purchased Gateway.
- In 2008, Acer purchased Packard Bell.

Computers aren't the only area in Technology battling maturity. Software, semiconductors, and consumer electronics markets, among others, are becoming increasingly mature.

FIGHTING MATURITY AND OBSOLESCENCE

When growth slows in a maturing industry, firms must find new ways to boost sales and earnings. Successful Technology firms have the following strategies to maintain or increase growth:

- Innovation
- Mergers and Acquisitions
- New Business Models
- Restructuring

Innovation

Innovation is at the heart of Technology, and one of the best innovators in the world has been California-based Apple Inc. The firm has a rich history of groundbreaking products, starting with the 1984 Macintosh. Apple's innovations in creating a user-friendly computer (as detailed in Chapter 2) helped propel the Mac to commercial success in a relatively new market.

But the computer industry soon became more saturated— Figure 5.2 shows US computer sales reaching a second peak in the mid-1990s (the first being in the 1980s), then moderating through the remainder of the decade. Growth has been relatively muted since,

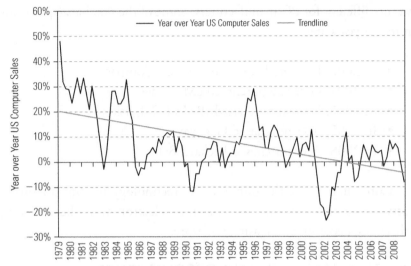

Figure 5.2   US Computer Sales Growth
Source: Thomson Reuters.

but this is the period in which Apple demonstrated its innovative strength.

Apple struggled during the early 1990s, losing market share as Windows-based PCs grew in popularity. In order to mimic PCs, Apple licensed its operating system to third parties. But too late—Windows already had a stranglehold on the computer industry. And by the late 1990s, growth was slowing.

Then Apple released a new kind of computer: The iMac G3. While not completely revolutionary, some distinct characteristics differentiated it from PCs—mostly physical design. Resembling early generation Macs, it was an all-in-one machine combining the monitor, CPU, disk drives, and ports in a single encasing. It was also aesthetically unique, with rounded edges and a transparent, blue-colored outer shell. These small yet innovative design tweaks revived sales. After reporting three years of falling sales, two of which included net losses, Apple sold approximately 1.8 million iMacs in 1999—a 68 percent increase over unit sales of similar products in 1998.[2]

Apple continued to find innovative opportunities to further expand growth in the highly competitive and saturated computer market. Next, it focused on peripheral devices that used computers as "digital hubs." In 2001, Apple released the iPod. Similar to the iMac, the firm focused on physical design, making the digital music player sleeker than the competition. It also continued its tradition of proprietary software aimed at creating a user-friendly experience. The iPod became a runaway success, eventually driving Apple's growth back into double-digit territory. Following its original release, Apple continually upgraded the iPod with increased memory, different colors, smaller sizes, and the ability to record and play video. Each enhancement and product refresh helped maintain growth and fight off market saturation. But, realizing the iPod's astronomical growth would not last forever, Apple made another innovative leap.

In 2007, Apple entered the mobile handset market. Combining its expertise in digital media players and user-friendly software, the company released its now highly popular iPhone. The device had a sleek physical design and unique touchscreen interface that was a departure from traditional mobile phones. It was an instant success, selling over one million units in the first 74 days of its release.[3] If fact, it was so popular that virtually every major handset producer in the world began manufacturing touchscreen devices. The iPhone eventually became Apple's primary growth driver, offsetting the slowing growth of its more mature iPods.

While Apple has enjoyed much success, overcoming product maturity is not an easy task. For example, Motorola was also considered an innovator. Its RAZR phone was revolutionary for its time, setting the standard for slim form factor mobile phones. It was highly successful, but like all phones, its growth eventually slowed. Motorola relied too heavily on the device and failed to produce innovative new models, resulting in significant market share loss and deteriorating growth. Motorola's stock was punished by investors.

So how does one invest on innovation? Unfortunately, there isn't a reliable way to tell what a firm has up its sleeve. Firms have a vested interest to keep developing products a close secret. One of the few methods investors can use is examining past performance, but this is a tricky game. Remember, both Apple and Motorola had a strong history of innovation. Only one, however, has yielded outperformance in recent years. So, while innovation can be a highly successful way of overcoming product maturity, it's highly unpredictable for investors.

Fortunately, for investors who manage their portfolios using a top-down strategy (discussed more in Chapter 7), long-term success is predicated more on getting higher-level themes right more of the time, rather than picking the right stock at precisely the right time—a very precarious undertaking. Further, when making individual stock decisions for a well-diversified portfolio, you may have the opportunity to hold several peers, increasing your odds of selecting the industry's better performers, rather than picking just one stock and hoping you get it right.

Mergers & Acquisitions

Another strategy Technology firms use to fight product maturity and slowing growth is acquisitions, and there are few Tech consolidators as successful as Oracle. The firm began and still dominates in database software—Oracle had a 44 percent share of the market in 2007.[4]

In 1995 and 1996, Oracle was growing sales by over 40 percent annually.[5] But naturally, as the market matured, growth slowed. After modest but healthy single-digit growth in 2004, Oracle purchased PeopleSoft for a final value of $8.4 billion.[6] The acquisition more than doubled Oracle's 2005 sales growth to 16 percent and broadened the firm's offerings in application software[7]—and kicked off an acquisition spree. In 2006, the purchase of Siebel Systems pushed sales even higher, and by 2007, growth was over 25 percent.[8] In just four years, the firm doubled annual sales, operating income, and net income. And Oracle's significantly expanded product portfolio generated cross-selling opportunities and helped reignite growth in its core database offerings.

Oracle's acquisitions have been successful overall, but offsetting product maturity through acquisitions can be risky. Integration can be costly, time-consuming, and potentially distracting to management. However, if done correctly and well, this strategy can bolster growth and strengthen a firm's competitiveness.

Buying Market Share and Global Presence

Another successful consolidator has been Taiwan's Acer—the world's third-largest PC manufacturer. The firm's operations have been extremely successful in Southeast Asia, but much of its recent growth has come from acquisitions. The first was its purchase of Gateway Computers in 2007 for approximately $750 million. This extended the firm's reach into the US, boosted market share, and propelled annual sales growth to 34 percent. In 2008, the firm expanded further into Europe with its purchase of Packard Bell, helping maintain sales growth above 30 percent. But despite its sizeable market share, the company is still relatively unfamiliar to US consumers. This is primarily because of its multi-brand strategy—the firm still sells PCs under the eMachines (owned by Gateway), Gateway, and Packard Bell brand names.

Source: Bloomberg Finance, L.P.

How does M&A impact the sector? It depends on how deals are transacted. When one firm acquires another by paying cash (either with cash on hand or with borrowed funds), the acquired firm ceases to exist as an independent, publicly traded firm. Those shares are removed from the market and sector share supply declines. Because stock prices are ultimately dictated by supply and demand, this should have a positive impact on prices if the demand for Technology shares remains constant or rises. This bullish force becomes more powerful if the sector as a whole experiences a high level of cash-based mergers.

But mergers can also be transacted in stock. For example, Firm A is worth $20 billion and Firm B is worth $10 billion—that's $30 billion in total stock supply. Say Firm A wants to buy B. Usually it'll pay a premium, maybe 20 percent—paying $12 billion. Firm A issues $12 billion in new Firm A stock, and B ceases to exist. Except, where we once had $30 billion in total stock supply, we now have

$32 billion. If this happens broadly, it can have a negative impact on prices sector-wide if demand for Technology shares doesn't keep pace.

Deals can also be transacted partially in cash, partially in stock. For example, Firm A might pay a hybrid of $6 billion in cash and $6 billion in stock for B. But most cash/stock deals tend to result in lower overall supply, which can be a bullish factor.

How do you know when cash-based deals or cash/stock hybrid deals are more likely to occur? Watch bond yields and earnings yields. A bond yield represents a firm's borrowing cost. The earnings yield is the reverse of the P/E ratio—the E/P (earnings per share over price per share). When earnings yields are higher than bond yields, a firm can borrow cheaply and buy a higher earnings yield—the difference between the higher earnings yield and the lower bond yield is profit. Done right, the deal finances itself and is immediately accretive to the acquirer's earnings. The acquirer's earnings per share rise, and, all else being equal, share price should follow. This is powerful incentive for CEOs to transact acquisitions (or buy back their own shares—the same concepts apply). Periods likely to see a higher rate of mergers and acquisitions are when interest rates are generally benign and bond yields are lower than earnings yields—just as we saw in 2005, 2006, and 2007.

That's the sector-wide impact, but the affect on individual stocks can be subject to other considerations entirely, at least in the short term. In the very near term, sometimes Wall Street reacts favorably to deal news, sometimes negatively. As an investor, it's critical you understand how a deal impacts a firm for the longer term and don't get swayed by near-term knee-jerk reactions. For a deal to work, firms should find targets that fit well into their existing business or somehow introduce a new, competitive value proposition.

New Business Models

Another strategy to battle mature or increasingly obsolete markets is shifting business models. This is more radical than the kind of innovation we've talked about so far. Instead of a PC maker innovating a new feature for computers, we're now talking entirely new product lines. However, doing this can be dangerous if it's a journey into the unknown.

One of the most successful transitions in business history was IBM's. After more or less creating the PC, IBM failed to recognize the market's potential and gave up control of the operating system and microprocessor to third parties in the early 1990s. Thanks in part to the rising strength of Microsoft and Intel, PCs gained significant momentum while sales of IBM's core mainframes fell. Corporate computer systems evolved, and, instead of the traditional all-in-one model, they were being pieced together with hardware and software from multiple vendors. This fundamental shift caught IBM off guard, bringing the firm to the brink of obsolescence.

Results suffered greatly. Between 1990 and 1993, IBM's gross margins fell from about 56 percent to 39 percent, with operating margins falling from 16 percent to 0.5 percent.[9] Mainframe sales were declining at a precipitous rate. The firm posted a net loss of almost $3 billion in 1991, which widened to over $8 billion by 1993.[10] The technology giant was nearing destruction, and its stock price fell almost 60 percent from the end of 1990 to mid-August of 1993.[11]

Many believed the firm couldn't survive as a vertically integrated organization, and then-CEO John Akers planned to split IBM into multiple independent companies—aiming to make them more nimble. However, after two straight annual net losses, Akers stepped down and the firm searched for a new CEO. In 1993, Louis V. Gerstner, Jr. became IBM's first ever executive from outside its own ranks, leaving his role as Chairman and CEO of RJR Nabisco.[12]

His first job was to return IBM to profitability, which meant significant cost reductions. In total, these cuts amounted to $8.9 billion, with 35,000 layoffs.[13] The firm reengineered operations, lowered expenditures, sold real estate and other assets, and reduced its dividend. By 1994, operating margins were back up to 7.8 percent.[14] However, this was only the beginning. Gerstner needed to make IBM relevant again, so he made a series of very large bets that challenged the way IBM previously operated.

The first bet was keeping the firm together instead of breaking it into pieces. Gerstner believed one of IBM's core strengths was its breadth of customer solutions.[15] The next two bets were on the future direction of the entire Technology sector. The growing industry trend was to build corporate computer systems with pieces from multiple manufacturers. A firm could use PCs from Dell, servers from IBM, and storage systems from EMC. However, it would be up to the firm's IT staff to figure out how to integrate the products, many of which operated on different standards. As a result, IBM bet Technology's future was in solutions helping customers build, integrate, and maintain these complicated piecemeal IT systems.

This last change didn't come easily. IBM now had to recommend competitors' products over its own if those products better fit the customer's needs. However, keeping the firm together proved a smart decision. IBM's deep expertise in so many fields of technology enabled it to offer a broad range of solutions. The firm also bet networked computing would overtake stand-alone, and that such a shift would require more open industry standards. As a result, IBM "opened" its products to interoperate with other industry platforms, which prepared it for the coming Internet revolution.[16]

IBM's turnaround did not occur overnight, but Gerstner was able to return the company to profitability in 1994 and increase net income almost 170 percent over the next 5 years.[17] Fast forward to 2008— IBM is now the largest IT services firm in the world. Operating margins are even back to 15 percent.[18] Though the firm was caught off guard, it successfully regained its footing by transitioning business models.

Because they all differ, there's no standard way to invest in new business models. Transitions can also take years to implement, which can reduce accuracy of forecasts. Also, as we'll cover in Chapter 7, it's impractical to make forecasts for more than the next 12 to 18 months, yet a wholesale change in a company's business model assuredly will take at least as much time, usually more.

However, performing high-level analysis on how a firm's strategy fits into wider industry or sector trends is always important. If you've determined the new strategy is a smart one, your next bet should be on execution. Can the company successfully make the transition? Can they do it faster than most expect? Answering these questions is difficult. Similar to the innovation example, looking at past performance is one of the few, albeit unreliable, ways to gauge competence. Experience is another. Who is leading the effort and is their background relevant? In IBM's story, Louis Gerstner had extensive experience running customer-centric organizations, which was particularly helpful as this was the quintessential focus of IBM's new strategy.

Restructuring/Cost Cutting

Another method of combating slowing growth is to restructure operations and reduce costs. This, however, is usually a temporary solution—getting leaner can improve profits, but it can't grow revenue. Without any catalyst to reignite sales, it may only slow bottom line bleeding. But if done in the face of increasing sales, it can add a significant earnings boost.

In recent years, Hewlett-Packard has been successful at cutting costs. While the firm has always made efforts to keep expenses in line, everything changed when Mark Hurd took the helm in 2005. Through an aggressive multiyear program, the firm cut its work force, overhauled its retirement plan, and continually streamlined operations. The results were impressive. After a 12 percent increase in 2005, operating income grew over 36 percent the following two years.[19] Margins expanded from 5.7 percent to 8.9 percent.[20] More notably, HP's stock price increased over 140 percent between 2005 and 2007.[21]

This stock appreciation was due to more than just cost cutting. In recent years, demand for notebook PCs skyrocketed, particularly from emerging markets. This benefited many firms, but HP was positioned particularly well with its better scale and superior global distribution network. Its stronger presence in regions with high demand led to market share gains over its closest rival, Dell.

EXTREME FLUCTUATIONS IN SUPPLY AND DEMAND

One common characteristic among Technology firms is enormous swings in product supply and demand and therefore prices—factors that can present significant challenges to growth or create large dislocations. These swings sometimes occur in new and emerging industries, but volatility is often higher in more commoditized markets requiring heavy capital expenditures—like Semiconductors and Semiconductor Equipment.

Semiconductors

Stiff competition and overly crowded markets have commoditized certain semiconductors (i.e., there's little product differentiation other than price). Demand for these chips often goes through boom and bust cycles, leading to wild gyrations in sales and earnings for the manufacturer—similarly impacting stock valuations. Typically, stock prices will tend to follow the same direction of the underlying commodity's price—in this case, the semiconductor. Hence, in an ideal scenario, product demand outstrips supply. This generally leads to higher chip prices—and stock prices—for all industry players, with some exceptions. The opposite can be said for periods of falling demand or chip prices. These periods, however, can cause irrevocable damage to certain manufacturers' sales and earnings and force them out of the market.

In recent years, one of the most volatile and fiercely competitive markets has been memory, specifically DRAM. The madness began with the announcement of Microsoft's Windows Vista in 2005. The new operating system required significantly more internal memory to function, leading many to believe its release would bolster DRAM demand. As a result, virtually all DRAM manufacturers increased production in order to meet this future surge in demand. There was just one problem: It never occurred—at least not at the level chip manufacturers expected.

The market flooded with DRAM chips and, naturally, prices fell. The decline was pronounced. As shown in Figure 5.3, from January

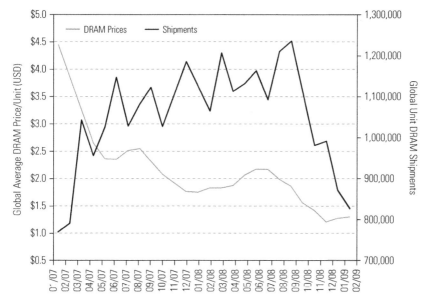

Figure 5.3   Global DRAM Prices vs. Unit Shipments
Source: Thomson Reuters.

2007 (when Vista was officially released) to January 2008 the average price per unit fell 61 percent, with an additional 28 percent drop the following year.[22] This is despite an upward trend in unit shipments that lasted until the Lehman collapse and sharp stock market sell-off in September 2008.

DRAM manufacturers were posting dismal results and stock prices suffered. Figure 5.4 shows performance of four global memory manufacturers. With the exception of Korea's Samsung Electronics, each company's stock price was down more than 40 percent from January 2007 to September 2008, before the Lehman collapse. Over the same period the MSCI World Index was down less than 10 percent.

Samsung outperformed its peers due to a few strategic attributes. First, it's the world's largest memory manufacturer with the widest economies of scale, allowing it to better withstand the negative pricing environment. Its stronger financial resources also helped it maintain higher levels of capital expenditure despite weaker profits. But perhaps

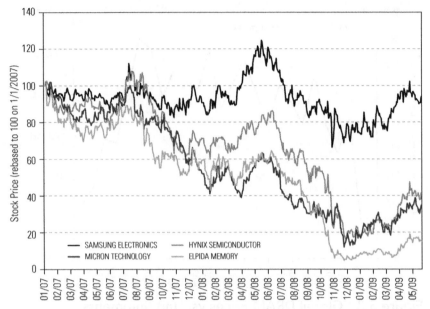

Figure 5.4   Stock Performance of Top Memory Manufacturers
Source: Thomson Reuters.

the most important attribute was its diversity. Samsung also happens to be the world's largest manufacturer of LCD panels and the second-largest mobile handset producer, behind Nokia.

Among many other macroeconomic factors, the severe pressure on memory manufacturers led to insolvency fears for certain players, some of which were realized. German memory producer Qimonda filed for bankruptcy in early 2009. (Counterintuitively, this led shares of remaining DRAM makers higher on speculation the supply decrease would drive prices for DRAM chips higher.)

Investing in volatile markets like DRAM is closer to investing in Materials or Energy firms than Technology. Stock performance is generally driven by price movements of the underlying product. In other words, you would expect the stock of DRAM producers to increase if prices for DRAM chips were rising (or expected to). Hence, the best method to invest in these types of markets is to generate forecasts on future product supply and demand.

Semiconductor Equipment

Semiconductor equipment is not commoditized in the same way as memory chips, but demand is heavily dependent on capital expenditures by semiconductor firms. When the semiconductor industry experiences volatility, so do equipment manufacturers. These capital expenditures are generally massive, so shifts in equipment demand can be violent. However, this volatility is cyclical and can act as both a headwind and tailwind at different points in the cycle. As covered in Chapter 3, semiconductor equipment stocks tend to perform best following deep troughs in the industry book-to-bill ratio.

DRAM market imbalances also impacted semiconductor equipment manufacturers. In 2006, chip makers were producing memory as fast as possible to boost supply in anticipation of Windows Vista. Many were even expanding production capacity by building new fabrication plants, leading to a significant increase in equipment demand. Top player Applied Materials posted 31 percent sales growth and 25 percent net income growth in its fiscal year 2006.[23] Moreover, 2006 fourth-quarter profit was up 82 percent, with memory manufacturers accounting for over 50 percent of total semiconductor equipment bookings.[24] It wasn't just Applied Materials that benefited—this was an industry-wide trend.

But DRAM prices started falling in 2007. To stem the decline, chip producers scaled back production and reduced supply growth. They reined in capital expenditures and ran plants at higher utilization rates, leading to a sharp fall off in equipment demand. After more modest growth in 2007, Applied Materials reported a 17 percent drop in sales and a 44 percent drop in earnings in fiscal year 2008.[25] The memory supply/demand imbalance had gone from a tailwind to a significant headwind in approximately two years, underscoring the importance of being mindful of potential supply and demand disruptions when analyzing Technology.

INTELLECTUAL PROPERTY THREATS

As detailed in Chapter 3, protection of intellectual property is vital for the ongoing health of Technology firms. Without strong protections, firms have little incentive to innovate or add to product lines. Yet, intellectual property is under constant threat—whether from different legal structures in foreign countries, illegal activity, or even normal competition—and it's a significant challenge for Technology firms to protect their intellectual property and their competitive advantage.

Piracy

Piracy is a common threat, most prevalent in emerging markets like China and Russia, where property rights enforcement is weak. The software industry has been one of the hardest hit—41 percent of all installed PC software in 2008 was illegally copied, a 3 percent increase over 2007.[26] This represents $53 billion in potential sales lost. It gets more expensive if you factor in legal costs to prosecute violators.[27] Companies like Microsoft have attempted to increase security features on products, but they never work perfectly. It is usually just a matter of time before violators find ways to circumvent protections.

Piracy can also be found in developed markets. While there is less actual counterfeit software, many take advantage of the "honor system" under which real software is sold. Businesses often pay for licenses on a per seat basis—a fee is paid for each terminal the software is installed. But in many cases, the software provider can't physically track the number of installations. They can only trust the customer will use it in a legal manner, which is not always the case.

Competition

Another challenge is property protection in Technology is less distinct than other sectors like Health Care, where small changes in chemistry yield completely different results. Technology competitors can more easily engineer around rules and emulate successful products. For example, Yahoo! built its search engine using a substantial amount of intellectual property, but the firm still couldn't keep Google from entering the market with a new, slightly different search engine. Apple's iPhone touchscreen is another example. Shortly after its introduction, almost every handset manufacturer introduced a similar touchscreen phone.

There are Technology firms that have successfully defended intellectual property, but success is never guaranteed. Until intellectual property rights are better defined, protecting them will be a continuing challenge for Technology firms.

Chapter Recap

Technology firms face a host of challenges. Finding ways to offset maturing or obsolete products is one of the largest. Firms use innovation, acquisitions, shifts in business strategy, and restructuring to maintain growth. There are also areas facing heightened volatility, and many firms are in a constant battle to protect intellectual property.

- Innovation is a primary lever of organic growth and market share expansion.
- There is no great way to forecast future innovation success other than by relying on past management performance and reputation. Buy innovation champions when you can get them at a cheap price.
- Mergers and acquisitions are common in the Technology sector. The best deals involve targets that are complimentary to current operations from a product or geographic perspective, come at a fair price, offer myriad synergy opportunities, and are margin accretive.
- Sometimes, firms in the Technology sector find themselves irrelevant and on the brink of obsolescence. In these cases, a complete shift in business strategy may be warranted, but it is one of the riskiest bets a company can make.
- Certain areas of the Technology sector have become increasingly commoditized. This has resulted in volatile demand and prices, which can act as both a headwind and a tailwind to Technology firms.
- Protecting intellectual property is a challenge for many firms in the Technology sector. This trend will likely continue in the absence of better defined property rights and enforcement.

6

A DEEPER LOOK AT CURRENT AND EMERGING TECHNOLOGIES

Technology is in a never-ending state of change. In the spirit of competition, companies pursue a common goal: Offer the best and most cutting-edge products or services possible. This has fueled the fire of innovation over the Technology sector's entire history. Advancement has been profound, particularly in the last 30 years, be it manufacturing processes, new products, or industry-wide technology standards.

This chapter digs deeper into some of the major technologies used today, as well as how they're evolving. For the semiconductor production process, some important emerging technologies include:

Semiconductor Production Process

- Immersion Lithography
- High-k Dielectrics

And emerging technology for computers include:

Computer Technology

- Solid State Drives
- Data Deduplication
- Cloud Computing
- Virtualization
- Web 2.0

SEMICONDUCTOR PRODUCTION PROCESS

Semiconductors have evolved remarkably quickly. Over the years, chips have dramatically shrunk in size while computing power has exponentially increased—a trend largely attributed to manufacturing process advancements. But just how are chips produced?

First Things First—Silicon Wafers

Chips start out as *silicon wafers*. Why silicon? Silicon is an abundant element, found in raw materials like sand, with natural semiconductor properties—meaning it can act as both a conductor and an insulator and be used at higher temperatures than many alternatives. (For more, revisit Chapter 2.) Because raw materials like sand and quartz are forms of *silica* (which contains oxygen), wafer producers must first source silica and strip away the oxygen in order to get purified polysilicon necessary for wafer production.

Silicon Valley

Silicon is the second most abundant element on Earth behind oxygen, making up over a quarter of the Earth's crust by weight.[1] The vital role this element plays in Technology lent a nickname to the South Bay Area in California. This wasn't due to a heavy supply of natural silicon, but to the significant concentration of semiconductor manufacturers located in the region—now known as Silicon Valley.

Polysilicon is then formed into *ingots*—crystalline cylinders. This is done by melting polysilicon down in a large crucible. A high-purity silicon rod is dipped into the mixture, and silicon crystals begin forming on the rod as it's rotated and slowly lifted from the mixture— forming an ingot (shown in the picture above). Ingots are sliced into thin wafers using a diamond saw blade, then smoothed and polished.

Wafers, measured in diameter, differ in size. The standard for much of the 1990s was 200mm, but most chip manufacturers have begun using larger 300mm wafers. The larger size allows more chips to be produced on a single wafer, improving manufacturing efficiency.

Producers are already beginning to talk about transitioning to larger 450mm wafers—odds are wafers will continue getting larger.

Chip Production Today

Once produced, silicon wafers are sent to semiconductor fabrication plants globally where they're used to manufacture chips. Chip production is a complicated, exacting process—done in a room free of dust and other particulates that can contaminate chips. The old Intel commercials with employees dancing around in space-like suits weren't off the mark—those futuristic ensembles are necessary to prevent skin particles and hair from entering the air.

Production is split into front-end and back-end processes. Included in the front-end are thermal oxidation, patterning, etching, and doping/diffusion—generally occurring in that order. The back-end is testing and assembly. The process itself (shown in Figure 6.1) generated over $42 billion in sales for Semiconductor Equipment firms in 2007,[2] with about 80 percent of semiconductor capital equipment spending on front-end equipment.[3]

Front-End Production   First, in *thermal oxidation*, silicon wafers are cleaned and heated to 1000°C in an oxidation furnace. The process forms a layer of silicon dioxide (insulator) on the surface of the wafer.

Patterning, often called photolithography or photomasking, is next. This is the step where circuit designs are imprinted on the wafer in a process very similar to taking a picture. The wafer is coated with

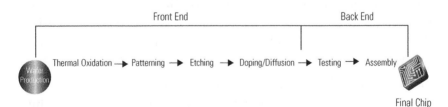

Figure 6.1   Stages of the Semiconductor Production Process

a layer of *photoresist*, or light-sensitive film. It's then placed under a *photomask*—a quartz plate containing microscopic cutouts of the circuitry. An ultraviolet light is then used to project the photomask's image onto the wafer where it's imprinted on the light-sensitive film.

How Low Can You Go?

A nanometer represents one-billionth of a meter. Typical human hair ranges from 60,000 to 120,000 nanometers wide. Red blood cells are 2,000 to 5,000 nanometers, and a strand of DNA is approximately 2.5 nanometers wide. Currently, the features on a semiconductor can be as small as 32 nanometers.

Source: National Nanotechnology Initiative.

Etching is the next step—the design imprinted on the photoresist is transferred to the actual wafer. This is done by hardening the image and etching away remaining portions of the photoresist with chemicals until only the circuit pattern on the wafer is left.

Once the circuit pattern has been successfully transferred to the wafer, its electrical properties must be altered—through *doping*—to make certain areas conduct electricity (the circuit pattern) while others insulate.

Doping and Altered States

How can you get a non-conductive metal to conduct? By *doping*.

In its natural state, silicon has four valence electrons. But conductive materials—like metals—have an odd number of valence electrons. The odd number allows valence electrons to flow freely from one atom to the next, generating an electrical current.

Silicon can be altered to conduct electricity by exposing it to *dopant* atoms such as phosphorus and boron—they need either one more or one less electron than silicon. The dopants are introduced to the wafer through diffusion or ion implantation.

In diffusion, the wafer is exposed to dopants in the form of a heated gas. In ion implantation, dopants are blasted onto the silicon wafer. Either process results in one extra or one less valence electron in the silicon atom—giving it the necessary odd number to carry an electrical charge.

The front-end production process is repeated for each layer of circuitry needed on a semiconductor device—some requiring over 20 layers.

Back-End Production   While not technically part of front-end production, there are a few additional steps before back-end production can commence. These are referred to as metallization/dielectric deposition and passivation. The former is a process where metal wires are used to connect conductive portions of the semiconductor and complete the desired electrical circuit. These metal layers are separated by dielectric films serving as insulators. The latter is the final step before back-end production. It involves depositing an insulating layer on the chip to protect it from contamination.

Back-end production is *testing* and *assembly*. Testing is performed on the entire wafer by automated computer systems. The wafer is then sliced into individual chips and defectives are removed. (The percent of functional chips on the wafer is referred to as the *yield*.) Remaining semiconductors are then visually inspected under powerful microscopes. Then, they're encapsulated into plastic, or sometimes ceramic, packages (*assembly*) and shipped.

EMERGING MANUFACTURING TECHNOLOGIES

At some point, Moore's Law (components on an IC should double every two years as features get smaller) may no longer apply—component growth will slow—due to sheer physical limitations (though scientists have been predicting such a slowdown for years, that's never come . . . yet). But where is the limit? This has been an ongoing issue facing chip manufacturers. However, new techniques have staved off the slowdown of Moore's Law—at least for now.

Immersion Lithography

The patterning phase has been particularly challenging in the quest to make ever-smaller features. Feature sizes on chips can only be as small as the circuit pattern imprinted on the wafer—done by shining light through a photomask. But features are already smaller than certain light wavelengths—traditional patterning methods have reached their limit.

The emergence of *immersion technology* extended the life of optical lithography. In traditional patterning, there's a gap of air between the light's lens and wafer surface—creating a physical limit to refraction angles. But water increases the number of angles. So semiconductor manufacturers replaced the gap with water instead of air, allowing further feature shrinkage and higher feature density on chips.

But once again, physics spoiled the party. Water has a refractive index of only 1.33—creating another barrier to resolution improvements.[4] The solution—using fluids and lenses with higher refractive indexes—eventually hit barriers, too.

The next solution was *double patterning*—the patterning phase is performed twice on a single layer of the chip, which can further reduce feature sizes. This technique allows manufacturing at the 32 and 22 nanometer levels[5]—*just 9 times wider than a strand of DNA*. The drawback? Double patterning—of which there are various forms, but all use two different photomasks—often doubles the cost.

So what's next in the world of lithography? *Extreme ultraviolet* (EUV) technology is one likely candidate (at the time of this writing). It involves a light source with a 13.4 nanometer wavelength.[6] At this point, this technique is still extremely challenging for manufacturers and widespread commercial use is likely years down the road. (Top litho-graphy equipment manufacturers include the Netherlands' ASML Holdings and Japan's Canon and Nikon.)

High-k Dielectrics

Dielectrics are materials that do not conduct electrical currents—more or less synonymous with *insulators*. They are a key component in semiconductors because they separate conducting portions of the chip.

Silicon dioxide is historically used in semiconductor production as a dielectric. But just as with lithography, problems arose as feature sizes shrunk. The space between wire interconnects and transistors (conducting portions) narrowed so much that silicon dioxide became ineffective. If the material was too thin it allowed electrical leakage, reducing reliability and significantly draining power.

In early 2007, after spending years evaluating hundreds of materials, Intel found a solution in a *high-k* material called hafnium.[7] (High-k stands for *high dielectric constant*—referenced by the Greek letter K.) These materials are thicker and can reduce electrical leakage by more than 100 times that of silicon dioxide.[8] Hafnium-based materials should allow further downscaling in the near term, but the laws of physics cannot be broken. One day a new technology will be required if feature sizes are to shrink further. (Intel is the pioneer and current leader in this technology, as of this writing.)

According to Gordon Moore himself: "It [Moore's Law] can't continue forever. The nature of exponentials is that you push them out and eventually disaster happens."[9] Semiconductor manufacturing may be closer to this limit than some think. The logical barrier would be when chip features approach the size of atoms—which is almost the case today. (One nanometer can be represented by a string of approximately 3 to 10 atoms.[10]) As of 2005, Gordon Moore believed it would be another 10 to 20 years before this limit is reached.[11] Only time will tell.

COMPUTER TECHNOLOGY

Be it PCs, servers, or storage devices, computer technology has reshaped and redefined how we operate as a society, creating efficiencies across virtually every business sector and driving significant productivity gains. And the computer evolution continues with a variety of emerging trends.

Emerging PC Technology—Solid State Drives

Though PCs come in many brand "flavors," they're all made with the same basic components—the microprocessor, motherboard, memory, hard disk drive (HDD), and liquid crystal display (LCD). PC evolution has largely been driven by advancement in these components.

Solid state drives like NAND flash have existed for some time, but they have a relatively new role in PCs—replacing hard disk drives as the primary form of storage. Capacities have yet to match hard disk drives, but flash memory offers some compelling advantages, like speed.

PC Components 101

Modern PCs are a sum of their parts—components often produced not by the OEM, but by other firms. (Even assembly can be outsourced.) Here are the most important components in building a PC.

Microprocessor—The central processing unit (CPU) is the computer's brain. It can have multiple cores on a single chip, which allows the CPU to perform multiple tasks at once more efficiently, improving performance.

Motherboard—CPUs are built into the motherboard, which is a platform for many parts and components. Not only does it include the CPU, but it also houses logic, memory, controllers, and passive components.

RAM (random access memory)—Part of a PC's main memory used to temporarily store data. It allows the computer to quickly access different programs without having to follow a specific order, hence the term "random."

DRAM (dynamic random access memory)—Common form of RAM. It is volatile memory that does not retain information in the absence of a power source.

Hard Disk Drive—Separate component containing a magnetic disk and reading/writing head. Storage capacities are vastly greater than DRAM or NAND flash, making these devices preferable for large amounts of data.

LCD (liquid crystal display)—Primary component of a PC's monitor in both desktops and notebooks. LCDs have replaced cathode ray tubes (CRTs) as the technology of choice because of advantages in size, weight, and durability.

NAND flash acts simultaneously as the hard disk drive and DRAM, improving speed and efficiency of accessing and running software programs. For example, computers using NAND flash as primary storage can boot up almost instantly. The downfall is limited storage capacity, but this continues to improve as Moore's Law is pushed further. Only time will tell if and when solid state drives completely replace hard disks. (Top memory producers include Korea's Samsung Electronics, Japan's Toshiba, and Korea's Hynix Semiconductor.)

Enterprise Storage Technology

Enterprise storage hardware can be deployed in multiple ways. Some businesses optimize their storage networks for speed, while others prefer a more seamless integration with existing hardware and software. All methods can offer some benefit depending on specific needs, but emerging technologies like *data deduplication* can help improve storage technology for all purposes.

Current Storage Network Standards   Storage systems can be set up in multiple ways depending on the type of computing environment. Direct-attached storage (DAS) was the first established. The key differentiator for this model is its absence of a storage network. For example, a hard disk drive on a PC can only be accessed by the PC it is attached to. On an enterprise level, the storage device might be connected directly to a server to boost that individual server's storage capacity.

In network environments, *network-attached storage* (NAS) and *storage area networks* (SANs) are currently the two primary and most commonly employed technologies. Both are a form of networked storage, but NAS incorporates file systems in the actual storage device itself, whereas in SAN the file system is separate from the storage device. Moreover, each utilizes different protocols and network standards for data transfer—NAS uses Ethernet while SAN uses Fibre Channel. The two are currently expected to converge into a new standard called *Fibre Channel over Ethernet* (FCoE).

Regardless of which environment is employed, the benefits are significantly boosted total storage capacity, allowing the sharing of information and resources across multiple end-users.

Emerging Storage Technologies—Data Deduplication   The most prominent recent breakthroughs in storage technology is in data management—a task performed by software. *Data deduplication* offers significant benefits regardless of a firm's underlying storage network technology (NAS or SAN).

Firms have a few ways to manage the challenge of a growing amount of digital data including *compression, file deduplication*, and *data deduplication*, with data deduplication currently being the most efficient. Compression removes redundant bits of file information to shrink that file's size. File deduplication removes entire redundant files. For example, an email attachment sent to 20 people in an office, when backed up, is stored 20 times on the storage hardware. File deduplication frees up space by removing these duplicate attachments.

Data deduplication goes further. If the attachment is a book chapter that is edited and forwarded on to others, who also make edits and forward it on, file deduplication only removes chapters that were exactly the same. But data deduplication looks at data in smaller blocks and determines what information is the same and what is different. It then removes redundant pieces of the chapter and saves one updated version in a single location. While compression might reduce storage by about 2 to 1 and file deduplication by about 3 to 1, data deduplication can reduce storage by about 20 to 1 or better.[12]

Data Domain and Quantum are niche players in this market. But at the time of this writing, EMC Corp. is acquiring Data Domain after outbidding rival NetApp—a reflection of this technology's value.

Other Notable Emerging Technologies

Computer technology is a highly diverse market evolving on many fronts. Out of the vast number that remain, cloud computing, virtualization, and Web 2.0 are technologies most worth mentioning.

Cloud Computing   "Cloud computing," a particularly hot emerging technology, is a fundamental shift from the historical computing model in which the user's PC housed the required software and hardware. In this new model, much of the required software and hardware can be stored in the "cloud" (i.e., the Internet). Each PC function can be provided by third parties as a service.

For example, computers could be manufactured without hard disk drives, DRAM, or even NAND flash. Instead, storage could be provided for a fee by firms like Google and Microsoft, which operate huge data centers with massive amounts of infrastructure. Even CPUs could be offered as a service. This is already occurring in the software industry. Software-as-a-Service (SaaS—covered in Chapter 4) is a form of cloud computing.

Cloud computing could cause PCs to grow "dumber"—evolving into simple Internet portals. Netbooks may be the first phase of this shift. The implications could be significant. Think of the music industry. Compact discs used to be industry standard (never mind vinyl records before them). However, the emergence of digital files like MP3s rocked the music world—music is packaged, sold, and promoted radically differently now—and the implications touched everyone in that world, from the artist themselves to their labels to the distributors to even concert venues and tour promoters. The long-form album was blown apart—consumers can buy single songs from any location with an Internet connection. Cloud computing has the ability to drive similar change in literally thousands of different industries, many of which fall outside the Technology sector. It can benefit businesses and consumers alike in time and cost.

But despite its many potential benefits, cloud computing has risks. For instance, is information stored at a Google data center more or less secure than if it were stored directly on company controlled infrastructure? Because of these risks, wide-scale adoption could take years.

Virtualization   *Virtualization* is software that helps improve hardware efficiency. It addresses a problem that began with the standardization of the client-server architecture. Under this model, firms often added separate servers for each additional application, many of which ran on different operating systems. The benefits were significantly higher computing capacity, but much of the hardware was underutilized.

Virtualization software can decouple the entire software environment from the hardware infrastructure, creating "virtual" instead of physical machines. Then hardware resources can be shared, regardless of different operating systems. The end result is significantly improved efficiency and utilization levels. Firms deploying virtualization software are often able to scale back hardware needs and reduce total IT costs. VMware is currently the leader in this market, but many others are jumping on the bandwagon, including industry giants Microsoft and Oracle.

Web 2.0   While better technology is enabling the transition, Web 2.0 is more societal than technology-based. The term refers to the so-called second phase of the World Wide Web. The transition has been underway for quite some time, but it is an ongoing evolution and a concept worth mentioning. The overriding theme is the transition from simple text and graphics to feature-rich multimedia content that can be generated and shared by all users, making the Web a more interactive and social medium (think YouTube, blogs, etc.). The transition, however, can create severe stress on existing network infrastructure due to the vast amount of content generated and shared (e.g., video). So while it may be difficult to pick out the next Facebook, investing in network equipment manufacturers is another way to ride the Web 2.0 wave.

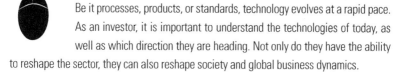

Chapter Recap

Be it processes, products, or standards, technology evolves at a rapid pace. As an investor, it is important to understand the technologies of today, as well as which direction they are heading. Not only do they have the ability to reshape the sector, they can also reshape society and global business dynamics.

- Semiconductor manufacturing is currently broken down into front-end and back-end production. Major steps involved include thermal oxidation, patterning, etching, doping, metallization/dielectric deposition, passivation, testing, and packaging.
- Immersion technology and high-k dielectrics are two emerging processes helping semiconductor manufacturers extend the life of Moore's Law.
- PCs differ by brand but maintain the same basic components. These include the microprocessor, motherboard, RAM, hard disk drive, and LCD panel.
- Solid state drives (NAND flash) are emerging as potential replacements for hard disk drives in PCs.
- Network attached storage (NAS) and storage area networks (SANs) are the two most common standards for enterprise storage networks. Each offers benefits depending on a company's specific needs.
- Data deduplication is an emerging technology within storage that helps firms optimize capacities and reduce costs.
- Additional trends to monitor in the Technology sector are cloud computing, virtualization, and Web 2.0.

III

THINKING LIKE A
PORTFOLIO MANAGER

7

THE TOP-DOWN METHOD

So if you're bullish on Technology, how much of your portfolio should you put in Technology stocks? Twenty-five percent? Fifty? One hundred percent? This question concerns portfolio management. Most investors concern themselves only with individual companies ("I like Microsoft, so I'll buy some") without considering how it fits into their overall portfolio. But this is no way to manage your money.

In Part 3 of this book, we show you how to analyze Technology companies like a top-down portfolio manager. This includes a full description of the top-down method, how to use benchmarks, and how the top-down method applies to the Technology sector. We then delve into security analysis, where we provide a framework for analyzing any company, and then discuss many of the important questions to ask when analyzing Technology companies. In the last chapter, we give a few examples of specific investing strategies for the Technology sector.

INVESTING IS A SCIENCE

Too many investors today think investing has a single set of "rules"— that all one must do to succeed in investing for the long run is finding the right set of investing rules. But that simply doesn't work. Why? All well-known and widely discussed information is already reflected in stock prices. This is a basic tenet of market theory and commonly referred to as "market efficiency." So if you see a headline about a stock you follow, there's no use trading on that information—it's already priced in. You missed the move.

If everything known is already discounted in prices, the only way to beat the market is knowing something others don't. Think about it: There are many intelligent investors and long-time professionals who fail to beat the market year after year, most with the same access to information as anyone, if not more. Why?

Most view investing as a craft. They think, "If I learn the craft of value investing and all its rules, then I can be a successful investor using that method." But that simply can't work because, by definition, all the conventional ways of thinking about value investing will already be widely known and thus priced in. In fact, most investment styles are very well-known and already widely practiced. There are undoubtedly millions of investors out there much like you, looking at the same metrics and information you are. So there isn't much power in them. Even the investing techniques themselves are widely known—taught to millions in universities and practiced by hundreds of thousands of professionals globally. There's no edge.

Moreover, it's been demonstrated investment styles move in and out of favor over time—no one style or category is inherently better than another in the long run. You may think "value" investing works wonders to beat markets, but the fact is growth stocks will trounce value at times.

The key to beating stock markets lies in being dynamic—never adhering for all time to a single investment idea—and gleaning information the market hasn't yet priced in. In other words, you cannot adhere to a single set of "rules" and hope to outperform markets over time.

So how can you beat the markets? By thinking of investing as a science.

EINSTEIN'S BRAIN AND THE STOCK MARKET

If he weren't so busy becoming the most renowned scientist of the twentieth century, Albert Einstein would have made a killing on Wall

Street—but not because he had such a high IQ. Granted, he was immensely intelligent, but a high IQ alone does not a market guru make. (If it did, MIT professors would be making millions managing money instead of teaching.) Instead, it's the style of his thought and the method of his work that matter.

In the little we know about Einstein's investment track record, he didn't do very well. He lost most of his Nobel Prize money in bad bond ventures.[1] Heck, Sir Isaac Newton may have given us the three laws of motion, but even his talents didn't extend to investing. He lost his shirt in the South Sea Bubble of the early 1700s, explaining later, "I can calculate the movement of the stars, but not the madness of men."

So why believe Einstein would have been a great portfolio manager if he put his mind to it? In short, Einstein was a true and highly creative scientist. He didn't take the acknowledged rules of physics as such—he used prior knowledge, logic, and creativity combined with the rigors of verifiable, testable scientific method to create an entirely new view of the cosmos. In other words, he was dynamic and gleaned knowledge others didn't. Investors must do the same. (Not to worry though, you won't need advanced calculus to do it.)

Einstein's unique character gave him an edge—he truly had a mind made to beat markets. Scientists have perused his work, his speeches, his letters, even his brain (literally) to find the secret of his intellect. In all, his approach to information processing and idea generation, his willingness to go against the grain of the establishment, and his relentless pursuit of answers to questions no one else was asking during his time ultimately made him a genius.

Most biographers and his contemporaries agree one of Einstein's foremost gifts was his ability to discern "the big picture." Unlike many scientists who could easily drown themselves in data minutiae, Einstein had an ability to see above the fray. Another way to say this is he could take the same information everyone else at his time was looking at and interpret it differently, yet correctly. He accomplished this by using his talent for extracting the most important data from what he studied and linking them together in innovative ways no one else could.

Einstein called this "combinatory play." Similar to a child experimenting with a new Lego set, Einstein would combine and recombine seemingly unrelated ideas, concepts, and images to produce new, original discoveries. In the end, most all new ideas are merely the combination of existing ones in one form or another. Take $E = mc^2$: Einstein was not the first to discover the concepts of energy, mass, or the speed of light; rather, he combined these concepts in a novel way and, in the process, altered the way we view the universe.[2]

Einstein's combinatory play is a terrific metaphor for stock investing. To be a successful market strategist, you must be able to extract the most important data from all the "noise" permeating today's markets and generate conclusions the market hasn't yet appreciated. Central to this task is your ability to link data together in unique ways and produce new insights and themes for your portfolio in the process.

Einstein learned science basics just like his peers. But once he had those mastered he directed his brain to challenging prior assumptions and inventing entirely different lenses to look through.

This is why this book isn't intended to give you a "silver bullet" for picking the right Technology stocks. The fact is the "right" Technology stocks will be different in different times and situations. You don't have to be Einstein, you just have to think differently, and like a scientist, if you want to beat markets.

THE TOP-DOWN METHOD

Overwhelmingly, investment professionals today do what can broadly be labeled "bottom-up" investing. Their emphasis is stock selection. A typical bottom-up investor researches an assortment of companies and attempts to pick those with the greatest likelihood of outperforming the market based on individual merits. The selected securities are cobbled together to form a portfolio, and factors like country and economic sector exposures are purely residuals of security selection, not planned decisions.

"Top-down" investing reverses the order. A top-down investor first analyzes big picture factors like economics, politics, and sentiment to forecast which investment categories are most likely to outperform the market. Only then, within those categories, does a top-down investor begin looking at individual securities. Top-down investing is inevitably more concerned with a portfolio's aggregate exposures to investment categories and factors than with any individual security. Thus, top-down is an inherently *dynamic* mode of investment because investment strategies are based upon the prevailing market and economic environment (which changes often).

There's significant debate in the investment community as to which approach is superior. This book's goal is not to reject bottom-up investing—there are indeed investors who've successfully utilized bottom-up approaches. Rather, the goal is to introduce a comprehensive and flexible methodology that any investor could use to build a portfolio designed to beat the global stock market in any investment environment. It's a framework for gleaning new insights and making good on information not already reflected in stock prices.

Before we describe the method, let's explore several key reasons why a top-down approach is advantageous:

- **Scalability:** A bottom-up process is akin to looking for needles in a haystack. A top-down process is akin to seeking the haystacks with the highest concentration of needles. Globally, there are 25,000 plus publicly traded stocks. Even the largest institutions with the greatest research resources cannot hope to adequately examine all these companies. Smaller institutions and individual investors must prioritize where to focus their limited resources. Unlike a bottom-up process, a top-down process makes this gargantuan task manageable by determining, up front, what slices of the market to examine at the security level.
- **Enhanced stock selection:** Well-designed top-down processes generate insights that can greatly enhance stock selection. Macroeconomic or political analysis, for instance, can help determine what types of strategic attributes will face head- or tailwinds (see Chapter 8 for a full explanation).

- **Risk control:** Bottom-up processes are highly subject to unintended risk concentrations. Top-down processes are inherently better suited to manage risk exposures throughout the investment process.
- **Macro overview:** Top-down processes are more conducive to avoiding macro-driven calamities like the bursting of the Japan bubble in the 1990s, the Technology bubble in 2000, or the bear market of 2000 to 2002. No matter how good an individual company may be, it is still beholden to sector, regional, and broader market factors. In fact, there is evidence "macro" factors can largely determine a stock's performance regardless of individual merit.

Top-Down Means Thinking 70-20-10

A top-down investment process also helps focus on what is most important to investment results: asset allocation and sub-asset allocation decisions. Many investors focus most of their attention on security-level portfolio decisions, like picking individual stocks they think will perform well. However, studies have shown that over 90 percent of return variability is derived from asset allocation decisions, not market timing or stock selection.[3]

Our own research shows about 70 percent of return variability is derived from asset allocation, 20 percent from sub-asset allocation (such as country, sector, size, and style), and 10 percent from security selection. While security selection can make a significant difference over time, higher-level portfolio decisions dominate investment results more often than not.

The balance of this chapter defines the various steps in the top-down method, specifically as they relate to making country, sector, and style decisions. This same basic framework can be applied to portfolios to make allocations within sectors. At the end of the chapter, we detail how this framework can be applied to the Technology sector.

Benchmarks

A key part of the top-down model is using benchmarks. A benchmark is typically a broad-based index of securities such as the S&P 500,

MSCI World, or Russell 2000. Benchmarks are indispensible roadmaps for structuring a portfolio, monitoring risk, and judging performance over time.

Tactically, a portfolio should be structured to maximize the probability of consistently beating the benchmark. This is inherently different than maximizing returns. Unlike aiming to achieve some fixed rate of return each year, which will cause disappointment when capital markets are very strong and is potentially unrealistic when the capital markets are very weak, a properly benchmarked portfolio provides a realistic guide for dealing with uncertain market conditions.

Portfolio construction begins by evaluating the characteristics of the chosen benchmark: sector weights, country weights, and market cap and valuations. Then an expected risk and return is assigned to each of these segments (based on portfolio drivers), and the areas most attractive are overweighted, while the least attractive are underweighted. Table 7.1 shows MSCI World benchmark sector characteristics as of 12/31/08 as an example, while Table 7.2 shows country characteristics and Table 7.3 shows market cap and valuations.

Based on benchmark characteristics, portfolio drivers are then used to determine country, sector, and style decisions for the portfolio.

Table 7.1 MSCI World Characteristics—Sectors

Sector	Weight
Financials	19.7%
Information Technology	11.7%
Energy	11.5%
Health Care	10.7%
Consumer Staples	10.5%
Industrials	10.3%
Consumer Discretionary	9.3%
Materials	6.8%
Utilities	5.0%
Telecommunication Services	4.7%

Source: Thomson Reuters; MSCI, Inc.[4] as of 12/31/08.

Table 7.2 MSCI World Characteristics—Countries

Country	Weight
US	48.5%
Japan	11.3%
UK	9.8%
France	4.8%
Canada	4.7%
Germany	3.6%
Switzerland	3.5%
Australia	3.5%
Spain	2.1%
Italy	1.6%
Hong Kong	1.1%
Sweden	1.1%
Netherlands	1.1%
Singapore	0.6%
Finland	0.6%
Denmark	0.4%
Belgium	0.4%
Norway	0.3%
Greece	0.3%
Portugal	0.2%
Austria	0.1%
Ireland	0.1%
New Zealand	0.0%
Emerging Markets	0.0%

Source: Thomson Reuters; MSCI, Inc.[5] as of 12/31/08.

For example, the Financials sector weight in the MSCI World Index is about 20 percent. Therefore, a portfolio managed against this benchmark would consider a 20 percent weight in Financials "neutral," or market-weighted. If you believe Financials will perform better than the market in the foreseeable future, then you would "overweight" the sector, or carry a percentage of stocks in your portfolio greater than

Table 7.3 MSCI World Characteristics—Market Cap and Valuations

	Valuations
Median Market Cap	$4,881 Billion
Weighted Average Market Cap	$57,374 Billion
P/E	9.7
P/B	1.7
Div Yield	3.8
P/CF	8.2
P/S	1.6
Number of Holdings	1693

Source: Thomson Reuters; MSCI, Inc.[6] as of 12/31/08.

20 percent. The reverse is true for an "underweight"—you'd hold less than 20 percent in Financials if you were pessimistic on the sector looking ahead.

Note that being pessimistic on Financials *doesn't necessarily mean holding zero stocks.* It might only mean holding a lesser percentage of stocks in your portfolio than the benchmark. This is an important feature of benchmarking—it allows an investor to make strategic decisions on sectors and countries, but maintains diversification, thus managing risk more appropriately.

For the Technology sector, we can use Technology-specific benchmarks like the S&P 500 Information Technology, MSCI World Information Technology, or Russell 2000 Information Technology indexes. The components of these benchmarks can then be evaluated at a more detailed level such as industry and sub-industry weights (as was done in Chapter 4).

TOP-DOWN DECONSTRUCTED

The top-down method begins by first analyzing the macro environment. It asks the "big" questions like: Do you think stocks will go up or down in the next 12 months? If so, which countries or sectors should benefit most? Once you have decided on these high-level portfolio "drivers" (sometimes called "themes"), you can examine various macro portfolio drivers to make general overweight and underweight decisions for countries, sectors, industries, and sub-industries versus your benchmark.

For instance, let's say we've determined a macroeconomic driver that goes something like this: "In the next 12 months, I believe global economic growth will be greater than most expect." That's a very high-level statement with important implications for your portfolio. It means you'd want to search for stocks that would benefit most from increased economic growth and activity.

The second step in top-down is applying quantitative screening criteria to narrow the choice set of stocks. Since, in our hypothetical example, we believe economic growth will be high, it likely means we're bullish on Technology stocks. This is because corporations tend to increase IT spending in strong economic environments. But which ones? Are you are bullish on, say, software? Computer hardware manufacturers? Communication equipment producers? Do you want producers with exposure to the US or another region? Do you want small cap technology companies or large cap? And what about valuations? Are you looking for growth or value? (Size and growth/value categories are often referred to as "style" decisions.) These criteria and more can help you narrow the list of stocks you might buy.

The third and final step is performing fundamental analysis on individual stocks. Notice that a great deal of thinking, analysis, and work is done before you ever think about individual stocks. That's the key to the top-down approach: It emphasizes high-level themes and funnels its way down to individual stocks, as illustrated on page 143.

Step 1: Analyze Portfolio Drivers and Country and Sector Selection

Let's examine the first step in the top-down method more closely. In order to make top-down decisions, we develop and analyze what we call *portfolio drivers* (as mentioned previously). We segment these portfolio drivers in three general categories: *economic, political,* and *sentiment.*

Portfolio drivers are what drive the performance of a broad category of stocks. Accurately identifying current and future drivers will

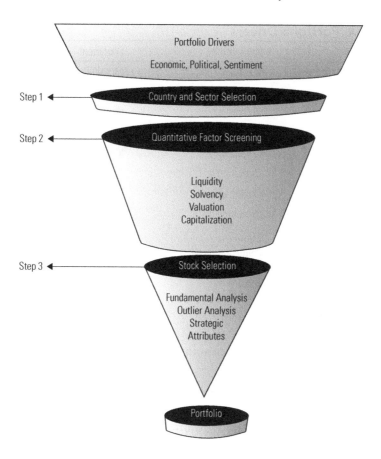

help you find areas of the market most likely to outperform or under-perform your benchmark (i.e., the broader stock market).

Table 7.4 shows examples of each type of portfolio driver. It's important to note these drivers are by no means comprehensive nor are they valid for all time periods. In fact, correctly identifying new portfolio drivers is essential to beating the market in the long term.

Economic Drivers   Economic drivers are anything related to the macroeconomic environment. This could include monetary policy, interest rates, lending activity, yield curve analysis, relative GDP growth analysis, and myriad others. What economic forces are likely to drive GDP growth throughout countries in the world? What is the outlook for interest rates and how would that impact sectors?

Table 7.4 Portfolio Drivers

Economic	Political	Sentiment
Yield curve spread	Taxation	Mutual fund flows
Relative GDP growth	Property rights	Relative style and asset class valuations
Monetary base/growth	Structural reform	Media coverage
Currency strength	Privatization	Institutional searches
Relative interest rates	Trade/capital barriers	Consumer confidence
Inflation	Current account	Foreign investment
Debt level (sovereign, corporate, consumer)	Government stability	Professional investor forecasts
Infrastructure spending	Political turnover	Momentum cycle analysis
M&A, issuance, and repurchase activity	Wars/conflicts	Risk aversion

What is the outlook for technology and infrastructure spending among countries?

Economic drivers pertain not only to the fundamental outlook of the economy (GDP growth, interest rates, inflation), but also to the stock market (valuations, M&A activity, share buybacks). As an investor, it's your job to identify these drivers and determine how they'll impact your overall portfolio and each of its segments.

The following is an example list of economic drivers that could impact portfolio performance:

- US economic growth will be higher than consensus expectations.
- European Union interest rates will remain benign.
- Mergers, acquisitions, and share buybacks will remain strong.
- Emerging markets growth will drive commodity demand.

Political Drivers Political drivers can be country specific, pertain to regions (European Union, OECD), or affect interaction between countries or regions (such as trade policies). These drivers are more concerned with categories such as taxation, government stability, fiscal policy, and political turnover. Which countries are experiencing a change in government that could have a meaningful impact on their economies? Which sectors could be at risk from new taxation or legislation? Which countries are undergoing pro-growth reforms?

Political drivers will help determine the relative attractiveness of market segments and countries based on the outlook for the political environment. Be warned: Most investors suffer from "home country bias," where they ascribe too much emphasis on the politics of their own country. Always keep in mind it's a big, interconnected world out there, and geopolitical developments everywhere can have implications.

What are possible political drivers you can find? The following is a list of examples that can drive stocks up or down.

- Political party change in Japan driving pro-growth reforms.
- New tax policies in Germany stalling economic growth.
- Protests, government coups, conflicts driving political instability in Thailand.

Sentiment Drivers   Sentiment drivers attempt to measure consensus thinking about investment categories. Ideally, drivers identify market opportunities where sentiment is different than reality. For example, let's say you observe broad market sentiment currently expects a US recession in the next year. But you disagree and believe GDP growth will be strong. This presents an excellent opportunity for excess returns. You can load up on stocks that will benefit from an economic boom and watch the prices rise as the rest of the market realizes it much later.

Since the market is a discounter of all known information, it's important to try and identify what the market is pricing in. The interpretation of such investor drivers is typically counterintuitive (avoid what is overly popular and seek what is largely unpopular). Which sectors are investors most bullish about looking forward and why? What countries or sectors are widely discussed in the media? What market segments have been bid up recently based on something other than fundamentals? If the market's perception is different than fundamentals in the short term, stocks will eventually correct themselves to reflect reality in the long term.

A note of caution: Gauging market sentiment does not mean being a *contrarian*. Contrarians are investors who simply do the opposite of what most believe will happen. Instead, find places where sentiment (people's beliefs) doesn't match what you believe is reality and position your portfolio accordingly. Examples of sentiment drivers include:

- Investors remain pessimistic about Technology despite improving fundamentals.
- Sentiment for Chinese stock market approaching euphoria, stretching valuations.
- Professional investors universally forecast US small cap stocks to outperform.

How to Create Your Own Investment Drivers

In order to form your own investment drivers, the first step is accessing a wide array of data from multiple sources. For country drivers, this could range from globally focused publications like the *Wall Street Journal* or *Financial Times* to regional newspapers or government data. For sector drivers, this could include reading trade publications or following major company announcements.

Remember, however, that markets are efficient—they reflect all widely known information. Most pertinent information about public companies is, well, *public*. Which means the market already knows. News travels fast, and investor knowledge and expectations are absorbed by markets very quickly. Those seeking to profit on a bit of news, rumor, or speculation must acknowledge the market will probably move faster than they can. Therefore, in order to consistently generate excess returns, you must either know something others don't or interpret widely known information differently and correctly from the crowd. (For a detailed discussion on these factors and more, read *The Only Three Questions That Count* by Ken Fisher.)

Step 2: Quantitative Factor Screening

Step two in the top-down method is screening for quantitative factors. With your portfolio drivers in place, this allows you to narrow the potential list of stocks.

There are thousands and thousands of stocks out there, so it's vital to use a series of factors like market capitalization and valuations to narrow the field a bit. Securities passing this screen are then subjected to further quantitative analysis that eliminates companies with excessive risk profiles relative to their peer group, such as companies with excessive leverage or balance sheet risk and securities lacking sufficient liquidity for investment.

The rigidity of the quantitative screens is entirely up to you and will determine the number of companies on your prospect list. The more rigid the criteria, the fewer the companies that make the list. Broader criteria will increase the number of companies.

How can you perform such a screen? We show two examples of quantitative factor screenings to show how broad or specific you can be. You might want to apply very strict criteria, or you may prefer to be broader.

Strict Criteria

- First, you decide you want to search for only Technology firms. By definition, that excludes all companies from the other nine sectors. Already, you've narrowed the field a lot!
- Now, let's say you only want European Technology stocks. By excluding all other regions besides Europe, you've narrowed the field even more.
- Next, let's decide to search only for Computer Hardware firms in the Technology sector.
- Perhaps you don't believe very small stocks are preferable, so you limit market capitalization to $5 billion and above.
- Last, let's set some parameters for valuation:
  - P/E (price to earnings) less than 12
  - P/B (price to book) less than 8
  - P/CF (price to cash flow) less than 10
  - P/S (price to sales) less than 10

This rigorous process of selecting parameters will yield a small number of stocks to research, all based on your higher-level themes.

But maybe you have reason to be less specific, and want to do a broader screen, because you think Technology in general is a good place to be.

Broad Criteria

- Technology sector
- Global (no country or region restrictions)
- Market caps above $10 billion

This selection process is much broader and obviously gives you a much longer list of stocks to choose from. Doing either a strict or broad screen isn't inherently better. It just depends on how well-formed and specific your higher-level themes are. Obviously, a stricter screen means less work for you in step three—actual stock selection.

Step 3: Stock Selection

After narrowing the prospect list, your final step is identifying individual securities possessing strategic attributes consistent with higher-level portfolio themes. (We'll cover the stock selection process specifically in more detail in Chapter 8.) Your stock selection process should attempt to accomplish two goals:

1. Seek firms possessing strategic attributes consistent with higher-level portfolio themes, derived from the drivers that give those firms a competitive advantage versus their peers. For example, if you believe firms with dominant market shares in consolidating industries is a favorable characteristic, you would search for firms with that profile.
2. Seek to maximize the likelihood of beating the category of stocks you are analyzing. For example, if you want a certain portfolio weight of Computers & Peripherals companies and need 4 stocks out of 12 meeting the quantitative criteria, you then pick the 4 that—as a group—maximize the likelihood of beating all 12 as a whole. This is different than trying to pick

"the best 4." By avoiding stocks likely to be extreme or "weird" outliers versus the group, you can reduce portfolio risk while adding value at the security selection level.

In lieu of picking individual securities, there are other ways to exploit high-level themes in the top-down process. For instance, if you feel strongly about a particular sub-industry but don't think you can add value through individual security analysis, it may be more prudent to buy a group of companies in the sub-industry or via a category product like an exchange traded fund (ETF). There are a growing variety of ETFs that track the domestic and global Technology sector, industries, and even specific commodity prices. This way, you can be sure to gain broad Technology exposure without much stock-specific risk. (For more information on ETFs, visit www.ishares.com or www.sectorspdr.com.)

MANAGING AGAINST A TECHNOLOGY BENCHMARK

Now we can practice translating this specifically to your Technology allocation. Just as you analyze the components of your benchmark to determine country and sector components in a top-down strategy, you must analyze each sector's components, as we did in Chapter 4. To demonstrate how, we'll use the MSCI World Information Technology Sector index as the benchmark. Table 7.5 shows the MSCI World Information Technology sub-industry weights as of December 31, 2008. We don't know what the sample portfolio weights should be, but we know they should add up to 100 percent. Of course, if you're managing against a broader benchmark, your Technology sector weight may add up to more or less than the Technology weight in the benchmark depending on over- or underweight decisions.

Keeping the sub-industry weights in mind will help mitigate benchmark risk. If you have a portfolio of stocks with the same sub-industry weights as the MSCI World Information Technology Index, you're *neutral*—taking no benchmark risk. However, if you feel strongly about a sub-industry, like Technology Distributors and

Table 7.5 MSCI World Information Technology Sub-Industry Weights vs. Sample Portfolio

Sub-Industry	MSCI World	Sample Portfolio
Computer Hardware	20.7%	?
Communications Equipment	17.8%	?
Systems Software	15.5%	?
Semiconductors	9.6%	?
Internet Software & Services	7.5%	?
Data Processing & Outsourced Services	5.7%	?
Application Software	4.3%	?
Electronic Components	3.2%	?
Office Electronics	2.9%	?
Computer Storage & Peripherals	2.6%	?
IT Consulting & Other Services	2.5%	?
Electronic Equipment & Instruments	2.4%	?
Semiconductor Equipment	2.3%	?
Home Entertainment Software	2.2%	?
Electronic Manufacturing Services	0.6%	?
Technology Distributors	0.3%	?
Total	100.0%	100.0%

Source: Thomson Reuters; MSCI, Inc.[7] as of 12/31/08.

decide to only purchase those firms (one of the smallest weights in the sector), you're taking a huge benchmark risk. The same is true if you significantly *underweight* a sub-industry. All the same rules apply as when you do this from a broader portfolio perspective, as we did earlier in this chapter.

The benchmark sub-industry weights provide a jumping-off point for making further portfolio decisions. Once you make higher-level decisions on the sub-industries, you can make choices versus the benchmark by overweighting the sub-industries you feel likeliest to perform best and underweighting those likeliest to perform worst. Table 7.6 shows how you can make different portfolio bets against the benchmark by over- and underweighting sub-industries.

Table 7.6 Portfolio A

Sub-Industry	MSCI World	Portfolio A	Difference
Communications Equipment	17.8%	22.0%	4.2%
Computer Hardware	20.7%	24.0%	3.3%
IT Consulting & Other Services	2.5%	5.0%	2.5%
Home Entertainment Software	2.2%	4.0%	1.8%
Computer Storage & Peripherals	2.6%	4.0%	1.4%
Electronic Equipment & Instruments	2.4%	3.0%	0.6%
Internet Software & Services	7.5%	8.0%	0.5%
Technology Distributors	0.3%	0.0%	−0.3%
Systems Software	15.5%	15.0%	−0.5%
Electronic Manufacturing Services	0.6%	0.0%	−0.6%
Semiconductor Equipment	2.3%	1.0%	−1.3%
Application Software	4.3%	3.0%	−1.3%
Semiconductors	9.6%	8.0%	−1.6%
Data Processing & Outsourced Services	5.7%	3.0%	−2.7%
Office Electronics	2.9%	0.0%	−2.9%
Electronic Components	3.2%	0.0%	−3.2%
Total	100.0%	100.0%	0.0%

Source: Thomson Reuters; MSCI, Inc.[8] as of 12/31/08.

Note: Portfolio A might be a portfolio of all Technology stocks, or it can simply represent a neutral Technology sector allocation in a larger portfolio.

The "difference" column shows the relative difference between the benchmark and Portfolio A. In this example, Portfolio A is most over-weight to Communications Equipment and Computer Hardware and most underweight to Office Electronics and Electronic Components.

In other words, for this hypothetical example, Portfolio A's owner expects Communications Equipment and Computer Hardware to out-perform the sector and Electronic Components and Office Electronics to underperform the sector. But in terms of benchmark risk, Portfolio A remains fairly close to the benchmark weights, so its relative risk is quite modest. This is extremely important: By managing against a benchmark, you can make strategic choices to beat the index without concentrating too heavily in a specific area and still be well-diversified within the sector.

Table 7.7 is another example of relative portfolio weighting versus the benchmark. Portfolio B is significantly underweight to Computer Hardware and most overweight to Data Processing & Outsourced Services and Technology Distributors. Because the sub-industry weights are so different from the benchmark, Portfolio B takes on substantially more relative risk versus A.

Regardless of how your portfolio is positioned relative to the benchmark, it's important to use benchmarks to identify where your relative risks are before investing. Knowing the benchmark weights and having opinions on the future performance of each industry or

Table 7.7 Portfolio B

Sub-Industry	MSCI World	Portfolio B	Difference
Computer Hardware	20.7%	0.0%	−20.7%
Communications Equipment	17.8%	15.0%	−2.8%
IT Consulting & Other Services	2.5%	3.0%	0.5%
Internet Software & Services	7.5%	4.0%	−3.5%
Systems Software	15.5%	13.0%	−2.5%
Computer Storage & Peripherals	2.6%	4.0%	1.4%
Home Entertainment Software	2.2%	4.0%	1.8%
Electronic Equipment & Instruments	2.4%	3.0%	0.6%
Technology Distributors	0.3%	10.0%	9.7%
Electronic Manufacturing Services	0.6%	0.0%	−0.6%
Application Software	4.3%	3.0%	−1.3%
Semiconductor Equipment	2.3%	1.0%	−1.3%
Semiconductors	9.6%	10.0%	0.4%
Data Processing & Outsourced Services	5.7%	30.0%	24.3%
Electronic Components	3.2%	0.0%	−3.2%
Office Electronics	2.9%	0.0%	−2.9%
Total	100.0%	100.0%	0.0%

Source: Thomson Reuters; MSCI, Inc.[9] as of 12/31/08.

sub-industry is a crucial step in building a portfolio designed to beat the benchmark. Should you make the correct overweight and underweight decisions, you're likelier to beat the benchmark regardless of the individual securities held within. But even if you're wrong, you'll have diversified enough not to lose your shirt.

Which again brings us to picking individual stocks—and Chapter 8.

Chapter Recap

A more effective approach to sector analysis is "top-down." A top-down investment methodology analyzes big-picture factors like economics, politics, and sentiment to forecast which investment categories are likely to outperform the market. A key part of the process is the use of benchmarks (such as the MSCI World Technology or S&P 500 Technology indexes), which are used as guides for building portfolios, monitoring performance, and managing risk. By analyzing portfolio drivers, we can identify which Technology industries and sub-industries are most attractive and unattractive, ultimately filtering down to stock selection.

- The top-down investment methodology first identifies and analyzes high-level portfolio drivers affecting broad categories of stocks. These drivers help determine portfolio country, sector, and style weights. The same methodology can be applied to a specific sector to determine industry and sub-industry weights.
- Quantitative factor screening helps narrow the list of potential portfolio holdings based on characteristics such as valuations, liquidity, and solvency.
- Stock selection is the last step in the top-down process. Stock selection attempts to find companies possessing strategic attributes consistent with higher-level portfolio drivers.
- Stock selection also attempts to find companies with the greatest probability of outperforming their peers.
- It's helpful to use a Technology benchmark as a guide when constructing a portfolio to determine your industry and/or sub-industry overweights and underweights.

Sub-industry is a crucial step in building a portfolio designed to beat the benchmark. Should you make the correct overweight and underweight decisions, you're likely to beat the benchmark, regardless of the individual securities held within. But even if some wrong, you'll have diversified enough not to lose your shirt.

Which again brings us to picking individual stocks—and Chapter 8.

8

SECURITY ANALYSIS

Now that we've covered the top-down method, let's pick some stocks, shall we? This chapter walks you through analyzing individual Technology firms using the top-down method presented in Chapter 8. Specifically, we'll demonstrate a five-step process for analyzing firms relative to peers.

Every firm and every stock is different, but viewing them through the right lens is vital. Investors need a functional, consistent, and reusable framework for analyzing securities across the sector. While by no means comprehensive, the framework provided and the questions at this chapter's end should serve as good starting points to help identify strategic attributes and company-specific risks.

While volumes have been written about individual security analysis, a top-down investment approach de-emphasizes the importance of stock selection in a portfolio. As such, we'll talk about the basics of stock analysis for the beginning to intermediate investor. For a more thorough understanding of financial statement analysis, valuations, modeling, and other tools of security analysis, additional reading is suggested.

Top-Down Recap

As covered in Chapter 7, you can use the top-down method to make your biggest, most important portfolio decisions first. However, the same process applies when picking stocks, and those high-level portfolio decisions ultimately filter down to individual securities.

Step one is analyzing the broader global economy and identifying various macro "drivers" affecting the entire sector or industry. Using the drivers, you can make general allocation decisions for countries, sectors, industries, and sub-industries versus the given benchmark. Step two is applying quantitative screening criteria to narrow the choice set of stocks. It's not until all those decisions are made that we get to analyze individual stocks. Security analysis is the third and final step.

For the rest of the chapter, we assume you have already established a benchmark, solidified portfolio themes, made industry or sub-industry overweight and underweight decisions, and are ready to analyze firms within a *peer group*. (A peer group is a group of stocks you'd generally expect to perform similarly because they operate in the same industry, possibly share the same geography, and have similar quantitative attributes.)

MAKE YOUR SELECTION

Security analysis is nowhere nearly as complicated as it may seem—but that doesn't mean it's easy. Similar to your goal in choosing industry and sector weights, you've got one basic task: Spot opportunities not currently discounted into prices. Or, put differently, know something others don't. Investors should analyze firms by taking consensus expectations for a company's estimated financial results and then assessing whether it will perform below, in line, or above those baseline expectations. Profit opportunities arise when your expectations are different and more accurate than consensus expectations. Trading on widely known information or consensus expectations adds no value to the stock selection process. Doing so is no different than trading on a coin flip.

The top-down method offers two ways to spot such opportunities. First, accurately predict high-level, macro themes affecting an industry or group of companies—these are your portfolio drivers. Second, find firms that will benefit *most* if those high-level themes and drivers play out. This is done by finding firms with *competitive advantages* (we'll explain this concept more in a bit).

Since the majority of excess return is added in higher-level decisions in the top-down process, it's not vital to pick the "best" stocks in the universe. Rather, you want to pick stocks with a good probability of outperforming their peers. Doing so can enhance returns without jeopardizing good top-down decisions by picking risky, go-big-or-go-home stocks. Being right more often than not should create outperformance relative to the benchmark over time.

A FIVE-STEP PROCESS

Analyzing a stock against its peer group can be summarized in a five-step process:

1. Understand business and earnings drivers.
2. Identify strategic attributes.
3. Analyze fundamental and stock price performance.
4. Identify risks.
5. Analyze valuations and consensus expectations.

These five steps provide a consistent framework for analyzing firms in their peer groups. While these steps are far from a full stock analysis, they provide the basics necessary to begin making better stock selections.

Step 1: Understand Business and Earnings Drivers

The first step is to understand what the business does, how it generates its earnings, and what drives those earnings. Here are a few tips to help in the process.

- *Industry overview.* Begin any analysis with a basic understanding of the firm's industry, including its drivers and risks. You should be familiar with how current economic trends affect the industry.

- *Company description.* Obtain a business description of the company, including an understanding of the products and services within each business segment. It's always best to go directly to a company's financial statements for this. (Almost every public firm makes their financial statements readily accessible online these days.) Browse the firm website and financial statements/reports to gain an overview of the company and how it presents itself.
- *Corporate history.* Read the firm's history since its inception and over the last several years. An understanding of firm history may reveal its growth strategy or consistency with success and failure. It also will provide clues on what their true core competencies are. Ask questions like: Have they been an industry leader for decades, or are they relative newcomers? Have they switched strategies or businesses often in the past?
- *Business segments.* Break down company revenues and earnings by business segment and geography to determine how and where they make their money. Find out what drives results in each business and geographic segment. Begin thinking about how each of these business segments fits into your high-level themes.
- *Recent news/press releases.* Read all recently released news about the stock, including press releases. Do a Google search and see what comes up. Look for any significant announcements regarding company operations. What is the media's opinion of the firm? Are they a bellwether to the industry or a minor player?
- *Markets and customers.* Identify main customers and the markets it operates in. Determine if the firm has any particularly large single customer or a concentrated customer base.
- *Competition.* Find the main competitors and how market share compares with other industry players. Is it highly segmented? Assess the industry's competitive landscape. Keep in mind the biggest competitors can sometimes lurk in different industries—sometimes even in different sectors! Get a feel for how they stack up—are they industry leaders or minor players? Does market share matter in that industry?

Step 2: Identify Strategic Attributes

After gaining a firm grasp of firm operations, the next step is identifying strategic attributes consistent with higher-level portfolio themes. Also known as *competitive* or *comparative advantages*, strategic attributes are unique features allowing firms to outperform their industry or sector. As industry peers are generally affected by the same high-level drivers, strong strategic attributes are the edge in creating superior outperformance. Examples of Strategic Attributes include:

- High relative market share
- Low-cost producer
- Sales relationships/distribution
- Economic sensitivity
- Vertical integration
- Management/business strategy
- Geographic diversity or advantage
- Consolidator
- Strong balance sheet
- Niche markets
- Pure play

Strategic Attributes: Making Lemonade

How do strategic attributes help you analyze individual stocks? Consider a simple example: Five lemonade stands of similar size, product, and quality within a city block. A scorching heat wave envelopes the city, sending a rush of customers in search of lemonade. Which stand benefits most from the industry-wide surge in business? This likely depends on each stand's strategic attributes. Maybe one is a cost leader and has cheapest access to homegrown lemons. Maybe one has a geographic advantage and is located next to a basketball court full of thirsty players. Or maybe one has a superior siness strategy with a "buy two, get one free" initiative that drives higher sales volume and a bigger customer base. Any of these are core strategic advantages.

- Potential takeover target
- Proprietary technologies
- Strong brand name
- First mover advantage

Portfolio drivers help determine which kind of strategic attributes are likely to face head- or tailwinds. After all, not all strategic attributes will benefit a firm in all environments. For example, while higher operating leverage might help a firm boost earnings in the booming part of an industry, it would have the opposite effect in a down cycle. A pertinent example to Technology is a vertically integrated semiconductor firm—or one that owns all of its fabrication plants. During periods of strong demand the company will have better control over output and run its plants at higher utilization levels. This reduces fixed costs as a percentage of total output and boosts earnings. However, the firm will bear the entire negative impact of low utilization levels during periods of slow demand, whereas a company outsourcing production would not. Thus, it's essential to pick strategic attributes consistent with higher-level portfolio themes and analyze those holding more importance in the current environment.

A strategic attribute is also only effective to the extent management recognizes and takes advantage of it. Execution is key. For example, if a firm's strategic attribute is technological expertise, it should focus its effort on research and development to maintain that edge. If its strategic attribute is its position as a low-cost producer in its peer group, it should capitalize by potentially lowering prices or expanding production (assuming the new production is also low cost) to gain market share.

Identifying strategic attributes may require thorough research of the firm's financial statements, website, news stories, history, and discussions with customers, suppliers, competitors, or management. Don't skimp on this step—be diligent and thorough in finding strategic attributes. It may feel like an arduous task at times, but it's also among the most important in security selection.

Step 3: Analyze Fundamental and Stock Price Performance

Once you've gained a thorough understanding of the business, earnings drivers, and strategic attributes, the next step is analyzing firm performance both fundamentally and in the stock market.

Using the latest earnings releases and annual report, analyze company performance in recent quarters and determine why. Ask:

- What are recent revenue trends? Earnings? Margins? Which business segments are seeing rising or falling sales?
- Is the firm growing its business organically, because of acquisitions, or for some other reason?
- How sustainable is their strategy?
- Are earnings growing because of strong demand or because of cost cutting?
- Are they using tax loopholes and one-time items?
- What is management's strategy to grow the business for the future?
- What is the financial health of the company?

Not all earnings results are created equal. Understanding what drives results will give clues to what drives future performance.

Check the company's stock chart for the last few years and try to determine what has driven performance. Explain any big up or down moves and identify any significant news events. If the stock price has trended steadily downward despite consistently beating earnings estimates, there may be a force driving the whole industry downward, like expectations for lower corporate IT spending. Likewise, if the company's stock soared despite reporting tepid earnings growth or prospects, there may be some force driving the industry higher, like takeover speculation. Or stocks can simply move in sympathy with the broader market. Whatever it is, make sure you know.

After reading the earnings calls of a firm and its peers (these are typically posted on the investor relations section of a firm's website every quarter), you'll begin to notice similar trends and events affecting the industry. Take note of these so you can distinguish between issues that are company-specific or industry-wide. For example, economic growth or higher component costs affect entire Technology industries, but import tariffs or government's tax policies may only affect specific companies.

Step 4: Identify Risks

There are two main types of risks in security analysis: stock-specific risk and systematic risk (also known as non-stock specific risk). Both can be equally important to performance.

Stock-specific risks, as the name suggests, are issues affecting the company in isolation. These are mainly risks affecting a firm's business operations or future operations. Some company-specific risks are discussed in detail in the 10-K for US firms and the 20-F for foreign filers (found at www.sec.gov). But one can't rely solely on firms self-identifying risk factors. You must see what analysts are saying about them and identify all risks for yourself. Some examples include:

- Stock ownership concentration (insider or institutional)
- Customer concentration
- Sole suppliers
- Excessive leverage or lack of access to financing
- Obsolete products
- Poor operational track record
- High cost of products versus competitors
- Late SEC filings
- Qualified audit opinions
- Hedging activities
- Pension or benefit underfunding risk
- Regulatory or legal—outstanding litigation
- Pending corporate actions
- Executive departures
- Regional, political/government risk

Systematic risks include macroeconomic or geopolitical events out of a company's control. While the risks may affect a broad set of firms, they will have varying effects on each. Some examples include:

- Commodity prices
- Industry cost inflation
- Economic activity
- Labor scarcity
- Strained supply chain
- Legislation affecting taxes, royalties, or subsidies
- Geopolitical risks
- Capital expenditures
- Interest rates
- Currency
- Weather

Identifying stock-specific risks helps an investor evaluate the relative risk and reward potential of firms within a peer group. Identifying systematic risks helps you make informed decisions about which sub-industries and countries to overweight or underweight.

If you don't feel strongly about any company in a peer group within a sub-industry you wish to overweight, you could pick the company with the least stock-specific risk. This would help to achieve the goal of picking firms with the greatest probability of outperforming their peer group and still perform in line with your higher-level themes and drivers.

Step 5: Analyze Valuations and Consensus Expectations

Valuations can be a tricky thing. They *are* tools used to evaluate market sentiment and expectations for firms. They *are not* a foolproof way to see if a stock is "cheap" or "expensive." Valuations are primarily used to compare firms against their peer group (or peer average) or a company's valuation relative to its own history. As mentioned earlier, stocks move not on the expected, but the unexpected. We aim to try and gauge what the consensus expects for a company's future performance and then assess whether that company will perform below, in line, or above expectations.

Valuations provide little information by themselves in predicting future stock performance. Just because one company's P/E is 20 while another's is 10 doesn't mean you should buy the one at 10 because it's "cheaper." There's likely a reason why one company has a different valuation than another, including such things as strategic attributes, earnings expectations, sentiment, stock-specific risks, and management's reputation. The main usefulness of valuations is explaining why a company's valuation differs from its peers and determining if it's justified.

There are many different valuation metrics investors use in security analysis. Some of the most popular include:

- P/E—price to earnings
- P/FE—price to forward earnings
- P/B—price to book
- P/S—price to sales
- P/CF—price to cash flow
- DY—dividend yield
- EV/EBITDA—enterprise value to earnings before interest, taxes, depreciation, and amortization

Once you've compiled the valuations for a peer group, try to estimate why there are relative differences and if they're justified. Is a company's relatively low valuation due to stock-specific risk or low confidence from investors? Is the company's forward P/E relatively high because consensus is wildly optimistic about the stock? A firm's higher valuation may be entirely justified, for example, if it has a growth rate greater than its peers. A lower valuation may be warranted for a company facing a challenging operating environment in which it was losing market share. Seeing valuations in this way will help to differentiate firms and spot potential opportunities or risks.

Valuations should be used in combination with previous analysis of a company's fundamentals, strategic attributes, and risks. For example,

Figure 8.1   Strategic Attributes & Valuation

below is a grid showing how an investor could combine an analysis of strategic attributions and valuations to help pick firms.

Stocks with relatively low valuations but attractive strategic attributes may be underappreciated by the market (as shown in Figure 8.1). Stocks with relatively high valuations but no discernible strategic attributes may be over-valued by the market. Either way, use valuations appropriately and in the context of a larger investment opinion about a stock, not as a panacea for true value.

IMPORTANT QUESTIONS TO ASK

While this chapter's framework can be used to analyze any firm, there are additional factors specific to the Technology sector that must be considered. The following section provides some of the most important factors and questions to consider when researching firms in the sector. Answers to these questions should help distinguish between firms within a peer group and help identify strategic attributes and stock-specific risks. While there are countless other questions and factors that could and should be asked when researching Technology firms, these should serve as a good starting point.

Software Industry

Revenues and Earnings Breakdown. How is the firm's revenue and earnings divided between businesses and consumers? Each is driven by different factors. Within the corporate market, are licenses enterprise-wide or seat-based? How much of sales and income are from licenses, subscriptions, maintenance, and support? This will reveal the firm's stability of operations and provide indicators on future growth.

Market Share. What is the firm's market share in each of its business segments? Does the firm have pricing power for its products and services? Implementing and learning new software platforms can be costly and time consuming, making switching costs high and entrenched customers valuable.

Research & Development. How much does the firm spend on R&D as a percentage of total sales? Software is a highly competitive industry characterized by constant innovation. A lack of compelling new programs or upgrades increases the chance of falling behind peers.

Upgrade Cycles. How long have the firm's products been available? When are new versions being released? Are features on new programs compelling? Will support for older versions be discontinued? New software programs generally carry higher price tags and can help boost top- and bottom-line growth. Discontinuing support for older versions often forces customers to upgrade.

Geographic Breakdown. What is the firm's geographic mix? Does the firm plan to focus on one region or expand geographically? Do its core competencies jibe with that strategy? Demand can vary considerably by region due in part to varying economic conditions. Piracy rates also vary by region and can negatively impact results.

Computers & Peripherals Industry

Revenues and Earnings Breakdown. How are sales and earnings divided between different business segments? Firms in this industry often have multiple product lines, some of which are more mature than others. This can help determine expected growth and whether the firm will be more profitable than its peers. Also determine if the company offers software or services. As more of its products reach maturity, additional revenue channels can help boost growth.

Gross & Operating Margins. This industry faces significant pricing pressure. Is the firm able to increase margins in a declining price environment? Does it offer compelling new products, and more importantly can it charge a premium for these products? Where are its manufacturing plants? Does it outsource? Labor costs can vary by region, giving companies with access to low-cost manufacturing an advantage.

Geographic Breakdown. What is the firm's geographic mix? Does the firm plan to focus on one region or expand geographically? Do its core competencies jibe with that strategy? Hardware saturation levels vary by region, and exposure to underpenetrated markets can often lead to superior growth rates. This can be crucial if there is little differentiation between products.

Distribution. How does the firm sell its products? Does it sell direct or use distributors? How is it positioned in the retail market? While no single category is always superior, some offer advantages given various forms of end-market demand. For instance, PC firms with a stronger retail presence would likely benefit from more robust consumer demand relative to enterprise.

Business Strategy. How does the firm maintain growth? Is it a consolidator? Is it expanding into new regions? Does it focus on being first to market with new innovations? Given the competitive nature of this industry, unique business strategies can be key in gaining market share.

Communications Equipment Industry

Customer Mix. Who are the firm's largest customers? Is it the dominant supplier to these customers? Does it have exclusive contracts with telecommunication carriers? Sales of infrastructure equipment tend to be bulky and tied to large capital expenditure projects. Knowing the firm's customers and network build out plans will provide insight into future growth. Success of a mobile handset is also highly tied to the wireless carrier offering it. How much will the firm spend marketing the device? How large of a subsidy is it offering on the phone? Is the carrier adding subscribers faster than peers?

Geographic Breakdown. What is the firm's geographic mix? Does the firm plan to focus on one region or expand geograhically? Do its core competencies jibe with that strategy? Levels of fixed-line and wireless infrastructure vary by region. Some markets are better for profits while others are better for top-line growth. This is especially true for mobile handsets. Sales of high-end devices tend to be stronger in developed markets while low-end devices tend to do better in Emerging Markets.

Innovation. How much is the company spending on R&D as a percentage of total sales? Does the firm have a history of being a first mover or does it typically chase peers? Does it hold any valuable patents? New trends in this industry happen fast. If the firm is not setting the standard, it must react promptly or risk falling behind.

Market Share. What is the firm's market share in each of its business segments? Does the firm have pricing power for its products and services? Moreover, can it pressure its component suppliers to lower prices? Market share often leads to leverage over suppliers and can create significant advantages in this highly competitive industry.

Inventories. How are the firm's inventory metrics trending relative to peers? Rising inventory levels could indicate the firm's products are obsolete and not selling well. The opposite could be true if the firm's inventory levels are declining faster than peers. But be wary, the firm could also be dumping older products into the market at reduced prices, which may negatively impact profits.

Regulation. How are the firm's operations affected by regulation? How might that change? Telecommunications is the single largest driver of sales in this industry. Telecom also happens to be an intensely regulated sector, and capital expenditures can vary in periods of favorable and unfavorable regulation.

Semiconductors & Semiconductor Equipment Industry

Market Share. What is the firm's market share in each of its business segments? Does the firm have pricing power for its products and services? How sustainable is its market share? The semiconductor industry is highly cyclical. Dominant players with larger scale are often better equipped to handle the industry's volatile nature.

End-Market Breakdown. What markets are the firm's chips sold into? How is demand trending in each? Are its end-markets diverse or concentrated? If it's an equipment maker, is it leveraged to the front end or back end of the semiconductor production process? What kind of chips do its customers make? Semiconductors are incorporated into virtually every electronic device, making these factors vital when reviewing both chip and equipment producers. Leverage to stronger end-markets can lead to better operational performance relative to peers.

Economies of Scale. Does the firm have more capacity than its peers? Is it the low-cost producer? How are its yields relative to peers? The ability to more efficiently produce chips on a large scale reduces fixed costs as a percent of revenue. A lower cost structure allows firms to price more competitively and gain market share.

Manufacturing Strategy. Does the firm do all of its own manufacturing or does it outsource production? Each strategy can wield advantages depending on demand conditions. During periods of high demand, a company owning all of its manufacturing facilities will have tighter control over production. It will be able to add capacity at will and benefit from higher utilization levels. A company outsourcing production would not have the same level of control and could unwillingly fall short of demand. The opposite can be true during periods of slow demand.

Supply/Demand Dynamics. How is product supply trending relative to demand? Are inventories building across the industry? Are chip manufacturers expanding production as prices fall? Several semiconductors have become commoditized where supply/demand dynamics are the single most important driver of price. Firms with large economies of scale tend to be better positioned in these environments. More advanced manufacturing techniques can also offer advantages over peers when there is little differentiation between products.

Technology & Innovation. What kind of advantage does the firm's equipment or chips offer relative peers? How much does the firm spend on R&D? Are its chips positioned at more advanced technology nodes (e.g., 45 nanometer vs. 65 nanometer)? Does its equipment result in higher chip yields? Maintaining the lead in technology is crucial to gaining market share. Manufacturing at more advanced levels also offers cost benefits as it generally requires less production materials.

Bookings. How are bookings trending relative to sales (book-to-bill ratio)? Is this ratio increasing or decreasing? This is especially important for equipment manufacturers. A company growing its book-to-bill ratio faster than peers may mean its products are in higher demand.

Balance Sheet. How are the firm's debt levels in comparison to peers? Does it have access to cheap financing? Manufacturing semiconductors is a capital intensive business. If a firm is overburdened with debt, it may not be able to expand capacity to meet demand.

IT Services Industry

Revenues and Earnings Breakdown. How are sales and earnings divided between different business segments? Who are the firm's customers? Does it have exposure to government spending? All of these are important questions as different forms of services have varying margin profiles. Governments can also be large spenders on IT services and generally represent stable sources of income. Moreover, governments often prefer domestic versus foreign providers for mission critical IT programs.

Corporate History. What is the firm's history and how long has it offered IT services? Does it have a track record of expertise in certain end markets? IT services can be used by any company in any industry. Firms with deeper experience in specific end markets will generally be better positioned for new business wins.

Geographic Breakdown. How large is the firm's geographic footprint? What countries and regions is it most heavily leveraged to? Global scale is becoming increasingly important in the IT services industry. Demand for payroll processing and related services is also highly dependent on employment environments, which vary by region. Additionally, some credit card and transaction processing firms fall into this industry. These companies are driven by consumer spending, which again varies considerably by region.

Competition. Who are the firm's major competitors? While this seems simple, many competitors are likely to come from other industries. Both hardware and software firms alike are moving into the IT services industry. For instance, IBM is classified as a hardware firm but also happens to be the number one global provider of IT services.

Internet Software & Services Industry

Market Share. What is the firm's market share in each of its business segments? Does the firm have pricing power for its products and services? How sustainable is its market share? What is the firm's share of page views and unique page views relative to peers?

Geographic Breakdown. What is the firm's geographic mix? Does the firm plan to focus on one region or expand geographically? Do its core competencies jibe with that strategy? Success in this industry is often determined by the number of users able to access the Internet. Penetration levels vary by region and companies with access to more users will generally have an advantage.

Brand Name. How strong is the firm's brand name? Does it vary by region? Switching costs are very low for consumers using search engines or content websites. A stronger brand name can help retain customer loyalty.

Traffic Acquisition Costs (TACs). What are the firm's traffic acquisition costs as a percentage of total advertising revenue? How does this compare to peers? TAC is indicative of a firm's scale, efficiency, and ability to monetize traffic on its website. In other words, is it becoming more or less expensive for the firm to bring in additional advertising revenue?

Regulation. How are the firm's operations affected by regulation? How might that change? Discussions surrounding Internet regulation have increased in recent years. Taking note of regulation in telecommunications is also important as it can have a direct impact on Internet firms.

Content & Services. This is a simple but important concept. Is the firm's content better than peers? If so, how is it better and can this be maintained? Does it offer a wider selection of products, better search technology, more third party vendors? How does it differentiate itself?

Electronic Equipment & Instruments Industry

End-Market Breakdown. What markets are the firms products sold into? How is demand trending in each? Are its end-markets diverse or concentrated? This industry is very broad and includes many companies that cannot be classified into other industries. Leverage to stronger end markets can lead to better operational performance relative to peers.

Customer Mix. Who are the firm's largest customers? Performance of many firms in this industry is ultimately determined by others. If it's a component manufacturer, what products are the components going into and is demand for those products strong? If it's a distributor, what products does it carry more of? If it's a manufacturing service provider, are its customers increasing or decreasing the level of outsourced manufacturing? Are these firms building new products or going through a refresh cycle? Understanding customers is vital in this industry.

Manufacturing & Distribution. Where are the firm's manufacturing locations? Labor costs vary by region and can mean all the difference in low-margin industries like outsourced manufacturing services. How many distribution centers does the firm have? Where are they located? For technology distributors, quick and easy access to customers is crucial.

Operating Margins. How are the firm's operating margins growing relative to peers? Technology distributors and electronic manufacturing services are both low-margin businesses. Those better at converting sales into profits can hold advantages over peers.

Office Electronics Industry

Revenues and Earnings Breakdown. How are sales and earnings divided between different business segments? Firms in this industry often have multiple product lines, some of which are more mature than others. This can help determine expected growth and whether the firm will be more profitable than peers.

Equipment Installations. How are the firm's equipment sales growing relative to peers? Majority of sales and profits in this industry are annuity based and include services, consumables (such as toner and ink), and financing. Equipment installations are a forward indicator of growth in these "post-sale" categories.

Research & Development. How much does the firm spend on R&D as a percentage of total sales? Office Electronics is a highly competitive industry characterized by constantly changing product portfolios. A lack of compelling new products increases the risk of falling behind peers.

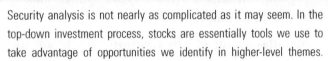

Chapter Recap

Security analysis is not nearly as complicated as it may seem. In the top-down investment process, stocks are essentially tools we use to take advantage of opportunities we identify in higher-level themes. Once an attractive segment of the market is identified, we attempt to find firms most likely to outperform their peers by identifying firms with strategic attributes. While the five-step security selection process is just one of many ways to research firms, it is an effective framework for selecting securities within the top-down process.

Do not limit yourself to the questions provided in this chapter when researching Technology firms—they are just some tools to help you distinguish between firms. The more questions you ask, the better your analysis will be.

- Stock selection, the third and final step in the top-down investment process, attempts to identify securities that will benefit from our high-level portfolio themes.
- Ultimately, stock selection attempts to spot opportunities not currently discounted into prices.
- To identify firms most likely to outperform their peer group, we must find firms that possess competitive advantages (aka strategic attributes).
- A five-step security selection process can be used as a framework to research firms.
- Firms within each industry have specific characteristics and strategies separating potential winners from losers. Asking the right questions can help identify those features.

9

UPGRADING YOUR PORTFOLIO—INVESTING STRATEGIES

This chapter covers various investment strategies specifically for a Technology allocation, building on the knowledge in this book. The strategies include:

1. Adding Value at the Sector Level
2. Adding Value at the Industry Level
3. Adding Value at the Security Level
4. Adding Value in a Technology Sector Downturn
5. Venture Capital

While the strategies presented here are by no means comprehensive, they'll provide a good starting point to construct a portfolio that can increase your likelihood of outperforming a benchmark. They should also help spur some investment strategy ideas of your own. After all, using this framework to discover information few others have discovered yet is what investing is all about.

Also, though these strategies focus solely on Technology, they are meant to be used as part of an overarching strategy for a portfolio managed against a broader benchmark. Some investors may choose to manage a portfolio *only* of Technology stocks (or any other single sector). But in our view, for individual investors, managing against a broader benchmark increases both risk management and outperformance opportunities.

STRATEGY 1: ADDING VALUE AT THE SECTOR LEVEL

Consistent with the top-down method, investors must first determine *when* it is appropriate to overweight or underweight the Technology sector relative to a broader portfolio benchmark. Some major factors contributing to this decision covered in depth in Chapter 3 are shown in Table 9.1. Each driver should be considered not on its own, but in combination with other relevant drivers and also larger macroeconomic conditions. Also, don't take this table to mean overweight decisions can be driven by the mere *number* of positive drivers

Table 9.1 When To Over- and Underweight the Technology Sector

Driver/Factor	Bullish	Bearish
Economic Environment	Expansion	Contraction
IT Fixed Investment	Strong	Weak
Consumer Spending	Strong	Weak
Component Shipment Growth	Increasing	Decreasing
Inflation	Slowing	Increasing
Equity Supply	Falling	Increasing
Technology Trends	Upgrade Cycles	
US Dollar versus Foreign Currencies	Weak	Strong
Tax Rates	Low or Falling	High or Increasing
Style Leadership	Growth	Value
Beta Leadership	High	Low
Sentiment		Euphoric

(and the same is true in reverse with underweight decisions). There can be, at any one time, many more meaningful drivers than we have space to list here. And some drivers are just more important than others. Most importantly, macroeconomic drivers can swamp sector, industry, and sub-industry drivers.

Implementing Sector Over- and Underweights

After the decision is made to overweight or underweight the sector, it's time to implement the strategy. The first step is determining the sector weight relative to your benchmark. The relative bet size should be proportional to your conviction. Mild conviction should translate to a more modest bet against the benchmark. The stronger your conviction, the bigger your bet. But a vital rule is to never make a bet so large that if you're wrong, you inflict irreparable damage to your portfolio's return versus the benchmark.

Next comes determining the actual investments. One method is directly mimicking the sector by buying all the sector's stocks in direct proportion to your under- or overweight. Obviously, this can be time consuming and costly—particularly for individual investors working with relatively smaller pools of money—depending on the number of stocks. An easier and likely cheaper method of mimicking the sector composition is buying Exchange Traded Funds (ETFs) or mutual funds. The following are some larger Technology ETFs:

- Powershares QQQ Trust (Ticker = QQQQ)—Mimics NASDAQ Index
- SPDR FD Technology (Ticker = XLK)
- Vanguard Information Technology ETF (Ticker = VGT)
- iShares DJ US Technology Sector (Ticker = IYW)
- iShares S&P GSTI Technology (Ticker = IGM)

For more on available ETFs, visit www.ishares.com, www.sectorspdr .com, www.masterdata.com, or www.invescopowershares.com.

STRATEGY 2: ADDING VALUE AT THE INDUSTRY LEVEL

A more advanced strategy is making industry-level bets based on your top-down analysis. Each individual Technology industry falls in and out of favor periodically—no one area outperforms consistently over the long term. Each will lead or lag the overall sector and even the broader market to some degree, depending on factors like corporate IT spending, consumer spending, upgrade cycles, stages of the economic cycle, and global or regional growth in end markets. Your job is to determine how pronounced the degree of leading or lagging will be, when it's likeliest to happen, and whether it's likely to be profitable enough to make a bet.

The performance of the MSCI World Technology industries from 1995 to 2008 (Table 9.2) illustrates the variability of returns. Calendar year industry total returns are compared to the Technology sector total returns. Shaded regions highlight industry outperformance.

The disparity in performance can be explained by some of the fundamentals, themes, and drivers covered in this book. Notably:

1. Software significantly outperformed from 1995 to 1998, coin-ciding with multiple operating systems' upgrade cycles.
2. Communications Equipment outperformed from 1997 to 2000 as telecommunications carriers spent heavily building out networks to accommodate increasing demand for Internet access and wireless service.
3. Electronic Equipment, Instruments, & Components, along with Semiconductors & Semiconductor Equipment, both outper-formed in the early stages of economic expansion (2003)—coin-ciding with demand for early stage components. Semiconductors & Semiconductor Equipment also outperformed following a bottoming book-to-bill ratio (2000 and 2001).

Ultimately, your decision to overweight or underweight an industry relative to the benchmark should jibe with your high-level portfolio drivers. Note: *Always remember past performance is no guarantee of*

Table 9.2 MSCI World Technology Industry Total Returns

Year	Internet Software & Services	IT Services	Software	Communications Equipment	Computers & Peripherals	Electronic Equipment, Instruments & Components	Office Electronics	Semiconductors & Semiconductor Equipment	Information Technology Sector
1995	N/A	29.3	52.1	27.8	28.5	11.5	20.7	N/A	31.1
1996	N/A	–10.8	48.1	20.2	27.3	2.2	14.9	N/A	28.6
1997	N/A	3.8	50.0	27.0	23.5	–6.0	13.8	N/A	23.1
1998	498.4	8.2	75.1	91.5	53.9	11.0	22.2	N/A	68.6
1999	155.3	54.7	84.3	142.7	66.9	162.5	–14.8	85.5	100.0
2000	–75.9	–41.2	–47.6	–38.0	–29.6	–41.9	–30.9	–30.7	–41.7
2001	–56.3	–23.3	–2.5	–55.9	–19.1	–39.3	8.5	–13.4	–29.6
2002	–47.7	–55.5	–28.6	–46.1	–33.9	–34.8	0.4	–46.2	–38.6
2003	147.3	25.1	24.3	66.8	34.0	49.2	30.2	84.5	48.3
2004	55.3	3.8	7.3	5.3	13.4	4.1	13.1	–20.4	2.5
2005	37.8	6.7	–1.5	2.1	–0.2	5.8	0.2	10.2	4.8
2006	–16.9	12.2	17.8	16.0	15.2	4.9	34.6	–4.1	9.3
2007	30.0	3.4	24.1	13.0	26.2	2.1	–9.8	4.5	15.1
2008	–53.3	–28.4	–38.4	–49.1	–41.7	–48.4	–37.6	–49.6	–43.9
Average Ann. Return	61.3	–0.9	18.9	16.0	11.7	5.9	4.7	2.0	12.7
Cumulative Return	124.9	–53.6	370.9	59.9	150.9	–34.7	38.3	–51.0	98.2
Standard Deviation	157.4	28.0	39.1	54.2	31.6	50.4	20.8	45.5	42.5
Beta (monthly returns)	1.2	0.4	0.8	1.3	0.9	0.8	0.2	1.6	1.0

Source: Thomson Reuters; MSCI, Inc.[1] 12/31/1994–12/31/2008.

future performance. No set of rules works for all time and you should always analyze the entire situation before investing. The past is about understanding context and precedent for investing—it's not a roadmap for the future.

Implementing Industry Over- and Underweights

Like implementing a sector strategy, industries can be over- or under-weighted by buying all the stocks in an industry proportionately, or by using ETFs or industry mutual funds. The following are some Technology industry ETFs:

- iShares S&P GTSI Software (Ticker = IGV)
- iShares S&P GTSI Semiconductor (Ticker = IGW)
- iShares S&P GTSI Networking (Ticker = IGN)

Industry Cheat Sheet

Sectors and their components are dynamic, and fundamentals change over time. But, for quick reference, the following is a cheat sheet with general pointers on each industry.

SOFTWARE

- Software has outperformed the broader Technology sector by the widest margin and in more years than any other industry since 1995. It's also a relatively large weight in most Technology benchmarks, so it's a good idea to hold at least a small allocation in any Technology portfolio to reduce benchmark risk.
- Outperformance tends to be driven by major upgrade cycles and periods of strong hardware demand (i.e., fixed investment referenced in Chapter 3).
- The industry also tends to outperform in periods of economic contraction (e.g., 2001–2002, 2008). While economically sensitive on the upside, it's also a defensive play as companies generate large percentages of recurring revenue through ongoing product support and maintenance.
- Given the relative stability of business models and outperformance during economic downturns, Software tends to lag in early stages of expansion and is more likely to outperform in mid to late stages.

COMPUTERS & PERIPHERALS

- Similar to Software, it's a relatively large weight in most Technology benchmarks, so it's a good idea to hold at least a small allocation in any Technology portfolio to reduce benchmark risk.
- Computers & Peripherals typically outperform during major upgrade cycles and periods of strong IT fixed investment.
- Falling component costs also help drive outperformance such as the 2006 and 2007 period when prices for memory and LCDs posted precipitous declines.
- This industry is another that holds up well during economic downturns. It consists of many large well-known conglomerates often perceived as less risky relative to smaller peers.

COMMUNICATIONS EQUIPMENT

- This industry can be thought of as "high beta." It's extremely volatile given its dependence on capital expenditures by telecommunications firms (which are typically large and lumpy in nature) and consumer spending.
- Outperformance often occurs in the early stages of economic expansion. Conversely, this is an industry to avoid during economic downturns.
- Outperformance typically coincides with rising capital expenditures in the Telecommunications sector—a trend clearly visible in the late 1990s with the massive investments in Internet infrastructure.
- Customers have a tendency to overbuild networks due to significant costs associated with upgrades (e.g., digging up streets to lay fiber) and to create excess capacity for future needs. This means the industry undergoes severe boom and bust cycles.

SEMICONDUCTORS & SEMICONDUCTOR EQUIPMENT

- This is another "high beta" industry with outperformance more likely in the early stages of expansion than late. Upgrade cycles, such as those within microprocessors, can also drive performance.
- Semiconductor Equipment can be extremely volatile due to its dependence on large capital expenditures by chipmakers. It tends to be driven by a combination of incremental capacity additions and advancements in underlying chip technology (e.g., shifts from 65 nanometer to 45 nanometer).

(Continued)

- Outperformance of Semiconductor Equipment tends to follow troughs in aggregate book-to-bill ratios, meaning it is best to be overweight during periods of improving orders.

ELECTRONIC EQUIPMENT, INSTRUMENTS & COMPONENTS

- This is a grab bag of firms leveraged to a wide range of drivers, including manufacturing cycles, construction, consumer spending, etc. This increases the difficulty of over- and underweight decisions as the aggregate industry is unlikely to be driven by a single focused driver.
- Performance is more related to broad increases or decreases in economic activity—it is best to overweight this industry in the early to mid stages of economic expansion and be underweight during contraction.
- Given its diversity, sub-industry and security level decisions can be more effective in generating outperformance.

IT SERVICES

- IT Services acts more defensively than other Technology industries. Business models are characterized by long-term contracts with recurring revenue streams, both of which help improve forward-looking visibility.
- Outperformance can most often be gained by overweighting the industry during economic contraction. While capable of outperformance during expansionary periods, it is rarer and generally to a lesser degree than other industries.

INTERNET SOFTWARE & SERVICES

- This has been the most volatile industry within Technology over the last decade, characterized by outsized returns in the late 1990s and a significant bust in the early 2000s (dotcom bubble).
- Advertising spending is a major driver of performance, which is also one of the more discretionary line items in corporate budgets. This means the industry typically outperforms during economic expansion (when ad spending is strong) and underperforms during contraction (when ad spending is weak).
- While this industry can generate significant outperformance, it is also the most volatile.
- Investors must remember that Google represents over half of the industry's weight (in the MSCI World). Hence, to make a bet on this industry is to also bet big on Google.

STRATEGY 3: ADDING VALUE AT THE SECURITY LEVEL

A still more advanced strategy entails investing directly in individual firms. This strategy could be based on different opinions about corporate IT spending, consumer spending, end markets, regions, or some combination of all the above. For example, if you expect strong demand for PCs to drive up DRAM prices:

- Focus on DRAM manufacturers operating at low utilization levels relative to peers, and avoid DRAM manufacturers operating at full capacity.
- Focus on semiconductor equipment manufacturers with heavier exposure to the DRAM market, particularly those with established customers already operating at full capacity.
- Focus on PC makers with the lowest cost structure relative to peers.

These are just a couple of examples, and they may not always prove correct—context matters. There are countless other potential tactics. As you become more familiar with specific Technology firms and their industries, you can eventually develop your own strategies. Always be vigilant for firm-specific issues that could cause a stock to act differently than you would expect in the context of your broader strategy. (And be sure to revisit Chapter 8 for how to select individual stocks.)

STRATEGY 4: ADDING VALUE IN A TECHNOLOGY SECTOR DOWNTURN

Most of this book focused on what drives the Technology sector and its industries forward. But what could cause a Technology boom to bust? No one sector or industry can outperform forever. The stock market eventually sniffs out all opportunities for excess returns, and sector leadership changes. So it's important to continually review all the drivers and question your high-level portfolio themes regularly.

Should your analysis lead you to believe the next 12 months will be a bad time for Technology stocks—because of the reasons detailed in Table 9.1 or something else—then it may be appropriate to either reduce or eliminate your weight in Technology firms or adopt a defensive position in your portfolio.

Implementing Your Defensive Strategy

If you have lower or negative expectations for the sector, you can:

- Get underweight by selling Technology stocks you already own.
- Short individual securities or Technology ETFs in an attempt to capitalize on an expected decline.
- While this should generally only be used on a short-term basis, you can purchase inverse ETFs such as the Proshares Ultra Short Technology (ticker: REW). These should rise in price if Technology stocks in general fall.
- Purchase put options on Technology stocks or indexes.

Because of the potential leverage involved, strategies involving options (which can be used either to augment an over- or underweight) and margin should *only* be used by sophisticated investors. Shorting is also a more sophisticated strategy. Keep in mind, significantly deviating from your benchmark involves the significant risk of missing equity-like upside should you be wrong; and, therefore, should only take place when you have strong convictions you know something others do not.

STRATEGY 5: VENTURE CAPITAL

Venture capital (VC) is the lifeblood of many nascent Tech companies. Its existence has been pivotal in shaping both the sector and underlying technologies used today, and it was one of the primary catalysts leading to the development of Silicon Valley. Giants like Intel and Google were backed by venture capital.

Investing in VC, however, involves different tools and analysis not covered in this book and is a very different process from buying stocks. VC firms are in the business of obtaining capital from investors to fund startups or fledgling companies, which in many cases are still in the idea stage. And most ideas don't pan out—research suggests only 1 out of 100 business plans that come in the door end up being funded.[1] But once an idea gets backing, the VC firm typically takes an active role in the development of the fledgling firm—with constant interaction with management and sometimes board representation.

Turning ideas into profit often takes years (if it happens at all), and during that period VC investments are generally more illiquid than common stocks. Profits are not typically realized until after the startup firm conducts an initial public offering or is acquired. In fact, additional funding is often required over the investment's time horizon.

Difficult to Predict

VC investments have risks common stock investors typically needn't consider. Much of this is tied to illiquidity and a lack of visibility. It's difficult for most investors to accurately forecast 12 to 18 months out, let alone the *8- to 10-year* time horizons associated with typical venture capital investments. There's simply too much uncertainty. Not only must VC firms generate assumptions regarding a business's viability and expected cash flows, they must also consider future market conditions years away.

Profits are gained only when investors can "exit"—liquidity events like an IPO or when the firm is acquired. And business is not always booming for M&A and IPOs—2008 is a great example. That year was characterized by a lack of liquidity and financial market instability. In fact, the total disclosed deal value for aggregate venture-backed M&A and IPOs fell about 63 percent from 2007.[2] Do you think VC firms saw this coming? Regardless, VC remains an integral part of the Technology sector and well-functioning capital markets.

Given the unique nature of VC, institutions are the primary investors—they're better equipped to handle the long-term time horizon, illiquidity, additional unique risks, and relatively high upfront costs. Typical investors include pensions, endowments, foundations, and corporations. However, it's not that difficult for high net worth individual investors to participate in VC funds.

GOOD LUCK!

We've covered a lot in these pages—Technology's basics, drivers, and common challenges. But remember, like all sectors, Technology is dynamic. The drivers and fundamentals vital today may not be tomorrow. But with the top-down method, you can apply a consistent framework to analyze the sector regardless of the current environment.

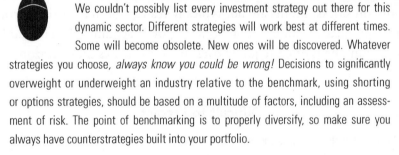

Chapter Recap

We couldn't possibly list every investment strategy out there for this dynamic sector. Different strategies will work best at different times. Some will become obsolete. New ones will be discovered. Whatever strategies you choose, *always know you could be wrong!* Decisions to significantly overweight or underweight an industry relative to the benchmark, using shorting or options strategies, should be based on a multitude of factors, including an assessment of risk. The point of benchmarking is to properly diversify, so make sure you always have counterstrategies built into your portfolio.

- There are numerous ways to invest in the Technology sector. These include investing in ETFs, index or mutual funds, or buying the stocks themselves.
- Investors can enhance returns by overweighting and underweighting Technology industries based on a variety of high-level drivers.
- An advanced strategy involves making bets on individual firms like DRAM manufacturers operating at low utilization levels relative to peers.
- Venture capital is the most direct method of investing in new technology firms. However, it is extremely risky and involves different tools and strategies than those required for stocks. It is also a market typically reserved for institutions.

Glossary

Note: The following are terms courtesy of the Semiconductor Industry Association's glossary. For more, visit them at www.sia-online.org.

3g   Industry term for third-generation wireless mobile communications networks.

56Kbps   The fastest speed modem that will work over a conventional dial-up phone line. Due to the FCC's mandated power limits, the maximum transmission speed of a 56K modem is usually only 53Kbps. Typical achieved transmission speeds average between 40Kbps and 46Kbps depending upon computer hardware, software, and line conditions.

A/D or DC   Analog-to-Digital Converter. This device is what all digital imaging systems use to get real-world pictures from a TV camera, for example, into a computer.

Analog Signals   Analog is a continuous signal, measuring features that are difficult to break into digital components, such as pressure, temperature, voltage, current, and air and water-flow. The circuits are used in products that involve sound (radios, TVs) and pressure (automotive air bags, anti-lock brakes).

Angstrom   One ten-billionth of a meter. Some chip layers are only 100 angstroms thick.

Application-Specific Integrated Circuits (ASIC)   Designed to suit a customer's particular requirement, as opposed to DRAMs or microprocessors, which are general-purpose semiconductors.

Application-Specific Standard Products (ASSP)   An integrated circuit that performs functions for a single application.

Assembly   A step in semiconductor manufacturing in which the chip (die) is either encased in a plastic, ceramic, or other package or assembled directly on a printed circuit board.

Bandwidth   An analog measure derived from the difference between the highest and lowest frequency on a carrier wave. Also used to describe the amount of data that can be sent through a given communications circuit.

Binary   Characteristic of having only two states, such as current on and current off. The binary number system uses only ones and zeros.

Bit   Binary digit. The basic unit of all digital communications. A bit is a "1" or "0" in a binary language.

Bluetooth   A wireless Personal Area Network (PAN) technology from the Bluetooth™ Special Interest Group, founded in 1998 by Ericsson, TBM, Intel, Nokia, and Toshiba. It is an open standard for short-range transmission of digital voice and data between mobile and desktop devices.

Broadband   Originally described the frequency bandwidth of analog circuits. The term has evolved to specify 56 KBps, then 1.5 Mbps capability.

Byte   A data unit of eight bits.

Cable   A term that refers to any of a number of wires or wire groups capable of carrying voice or data transmissions.

Chip   An individual integrated circuit built in a tiny, layered rectangle or square on a silicon wafer.

Circuit Board   Same as printed circuit board. A board with microprocessors, transistors, and other electronic components. Also called a circuit card.

Cleanroom   The sterile rooms where chips are fabricated. The air in these rooms is thousands of times cleaner than in a typical hospital operating room.

Code Division Multiple Access (CDMA)   Also called Spread Spectrum, a term for a form of digital spread spectrum cellular phone service that assigns a code to all speech bits, sends a scrambled transmission of the encoded speech over the air, and reassembles the speech into its original format. CDMA has up to 20 times the capacity of analog cellular service and is best known for its superior call quality and long battery life.

Computer-Aided Design (CAD)   Sophisticated, computerized workstations and software used to design integrated circuit chips.

Defect A chemical or structural irregularity that degrades the product. Defects can affect the product over time or interfere with manufacturing the chip correctly. Common causes of defects are flakes from skin or cosmetics and droplets from a person's sneeze.

Die A single integrated circuit (or chip) cut from the wafer on which it was manufactured.

Digital The method of representing information as numbers with discrete (non-continuous) values, usually expressed as a sequence of binary digits (ones and zeros).

Digital Cellular State of the art in cellular communications technology, up to 15 times the capacity of analog technology with significantly less static, loss/interruption of the signal when passing between cells, and connection problems because of congested relays.

Digital Modem A term given to a piece of equipment that joins a digital phone line to a phone, PC, or other hardware. It allows for testing, conditioning, circuit timing, and other analysis of a phone line and is not used for communications purposes.

Digital Signal Processing (DSP) Digital circuits designed to address a broad class of problems in signal reception and analysis that have traditionally been solved using analog components. DSP is used to enhance, analyze, filter, modulate, or otherwise manipulate standard analog functions, such as images, sounds, radar pulses, and other such signals by analyzing and transforming wave-forms (e.g., transmitting data over phone lines via modem).

Digital Subscriber Line (DSL) A technology that increases the digital speed of ordinary phone lines by a substantial factor over common dial-up modems. Offers symmetrical and asymmetrical operation. Asymmetrical versions (ADSL, RADSL, VDSL, etc.) provide higher downstream transmission than upstream and are better suited for Internet usage and video on demand applications. Symmetric DLS (HDLS, SDSL, IDSL, etc.) provide the same speed in both directions. All DSLs have distance limitations of around two or three miles between the telephone company's central office and the customer site.

Diode A signal and switching device that allows current in one direction and blocks it in the opposite direction. One use: regulating load voltages.

Discrete Device A device that contains one active element, such as a transistor or diode, although a hybrid might contain more than one active element. In comparison, an integrated circuit could contain millions of active elements on a single chip.

Doping A wafer fabrication process in which exposed areas of silicon are bombarded with chemical impurities to alter the way the silicon conducts electricity in those areas.

Dynamic Random Access Memory (DRAM) A type of memory component. "Dynamic" means the device's memory cells must be recharged periodically. Information stored in the memory cells is accessed randomly. Memory is a key component of most electronic products.

Embedded Processor A computer chip that controls the function of its product. While embedded processors sometimes refer to the type of chips used in simple electronic toys, "talking" greeting cards, and similar consumer products, they are also high-functioning microcontrollers that are the brains of products such as laser printers.

Etch The removal of selected portions of materials to define patterned layers on chips.

Ethernet A local area network used for connecting computer, printers, workstations, terminals, servers, and other computer hardware within the same company. Ethernet operates over twisted wire and over coaxial cable at speeds up to 10 million bits per second (Mbps).

Extreme Ultraviolet Technology (EUV) A technology for extending ultraviolet lithography by manufacturing a lens with concave and convex mirrors. This type of manufacturing allows the lens to focus patterns on a chip that are too small to be lithographed.

Fab The fabrication facility, or fab, is the manufacturing plant where the front-end process of making semiconductors on silicon wafers is completed. The package and assembly (back-end) stages are typically completed at other facilities.

Fabless A semiconductor company with no wafer fabrication capability.

Foundry A wafer production and processing plant. Usually used to denote a facility that is available on a contract basis to companies that do not have wafer fab capability of their own, or that wish to supplement their own capabilities.

Integrated Circuit (IC) Semiconductor chip in which many active or passive elements are fabricated and connected together on a continuous substrate, as opposed to discrete devices, such as transistors, resistors, capacitors, and diodes that exist individually.

Ion Implantation   One way that the surface of a chip is transformed. It is a method that fires beams of charged atoms at the surface of the wafer. The high level of energy of these ions allows them to penetrate the silicon to produce the desired doping effect.

Lithography   The transfer of a pattern or image from one medium to another, as from a mask to a wafer. If light is used to effect the transfer, the term "photolithography" applies. "Microlithography" refers to the process as applied to images with features in the micrometer range.

Local Area Network (LAN)   A communications network that serves users within a confined geographical area and is made up of servers, workstations, a network operating system, and a communications link.

Microcontroller   A microcontroller is a stand-alone device that performs computer functions within an electronic system without the need of other support circuits. A microcontroller contains memory functions, unlike a microprocessor, which is typically paired with a chip that provides memory. Microcontrollers are used in TVs, VCRs, microwave ovens, and automobile engines.

Micron   A metric unit of linear measure that equals one millionth of a meter or one thousandth of a millimeter. A thousand times bigger than a nanometer. The diameter of a human hair is about 100 microns. Today's semiconductors have lines etched at .18 microns.

Microprocessor   A central processing unit (CPU) fabricated on one or more chips, containing the basic arithmetic, logic, and control elements required by a computer for processing data. Microprocessor also refers to an integrated circuit that accepts coded instructions, executes the instructions, and delivers signals that describe its internal status.

Mixed Signals   A class of ICs that have traditionally been considered analog semiconductors. They can also be defined as anything that combines analog and digital circuitry—and that includes many ASICs and DSPs.

Modem   A type of computer equipment that links computers via telephone lines and enables the transmission of data. Derived from the words "modulate" and "demodulate," because a modem converts, or modulates, transmission signals from digital to analog for transmission over analog telecommunications lines, and then converts them back, or demodulates the signals, from analog back to digital.

Nanometer   A metric unit of linear measure that equals one billionth of a meter.

Nanotechnology   The ability to see, measure, and make objects that are within the same tiny size scale as atoms and molecules. The nanotechnology realm can be defined as being between 0.1 nanometer (about the size of a hydrogen atom) and 100 nanometers (about the size of a virus).

Network   An arrangement of objects that are interconnected. In communications, the transmission channels interconnecting all clients and server stations as well as all supporting hardware and software.

Non-Volatile Memory   A storage device whose contents are preserved when its power is off. Storage using magnetic disks or tape is normally non-volatile. Some semiconductor memories (ROM, EPROM, Flash memory) are non-volatile while other semiconductor memories (static RAM and especially dynamic RAM) are normally volatile but can be made into non-volatile storage by permanently connecting a (rechargeable) battery.

Optoelectronics   A device that is responsive to or that emits or modifies light waves. Examples are LEDs, optical couplers, laser diodes, and photo detectors.

Packaging   The protective container or housing for an electronic component or die, with external terminals to provide electrical access to the components inside. Packages provide for power and signal distribution, power dissipation, and physical and chemical protection of the circuits.

Printed Circuit Board (PCB)   Flat material on which electronic components are mounted. Also provides electrical pathways that connect components.

Radio Frequency (RF)   The rage of electromagnetic frequencies above the audio range and below the visible light. All broadcast transmission, from AM radio to satellites, falls into this range, between 30KHz and 300GHz.

Random Access Memory (RAM)   May be written to, or read from, any address location in any sequence. Also called a read/write memory, RAM stores digital bits temporarily and can be changed rapidly as required. RAM constitutes the basic read/write storage element in computers.

Semiconductor   This is the generic name for discrete devices and integrated circuits that can control the flow of electrical signals. Silicon is the basic material on which semiconductors are fabricated.

Solid State   Refers to the electronic properties of crystalline material, as opposed to vacuum and gas-filled tubes that transmit electricity. Compared with earlier vacuum-tube devices, solid-state components are smaller, less expensive, more reliable, use less power, and generate less heat.

Substrate   The body or base layer of an integrated circuit, onto which other layers are deposited to form the circuit. The substrate is usually silicon, although sapphire is used for certain applications, particularly military, where radiation resistance is important. The substrate is originally part of the wafer from which the die is cut. It is used as the electrical ground for the circuit.

System on a Chip   A chip that is a self-contained system, including processing, memory, and input-output functions.

Transistor   An electronic device capable of amplifying electronic signals similar to the vacuum tube but made from a semiconductor material such as silicon or germanium.

Wafer   A thin slice, typically 10 to 30 mils thick, sawed from a cylindrical ingot (boule) of extremely pure, crystalline silicon, typically six to eight inches in diameter. Arrays of ICs or discrete devices are fabricated in the wafers during the manufacturing process.

Yield   Yield refers to the percentage or absolute number of defect-free die on a silicon wafer or of packaged units that pass all device specifications. Because it costs the same to process a wafer with 10 percent good die as 90 percent good die, eliminating defects and improving yield become the critical variable in determining the cost per chip.

Notes

CHAPTER 1: TECHNOLOGY BASICS

1. Semiconductor Industry Association, "Global Chip Sales Hit $225.6 Billion in 2007," (February 1, 2008), http://www.sia-online.org/cs/papers_publications/press_release_detail?pressrelease.id=1497 (accessed July 21, 2009).
2. Semiconductor Industry Association, "Worldwide Market Billings," (September 2008), http://www.sia-online.org/galleries/Statistics/GSR1976-September08.xls (accessed July 21, 2009).
3. Ibid.
4. iSuppli Applied Market Intelligence, "Notebook PC Shipments Exceed Desktop for First Time in Q3," (December 29, 2008), http://www.isuppli.com/MarketWatchDetail. aspx?ID=318 (accessed July 21, 2009).
5. IBM, "Introduction to the New Mainframe: z/OS Basics," (July 2006), http://publibz .boulder.ibm.com/zoslib/pdf/zosbasic.pdf?bcsi_scan_408DE456E3075246=1 (accessed July 21, 2009).
6. Blade.org, "Blade Server Technology Overview," http://www.blade.org/techover.cfm (accessed July 21, 2009).
7. John Markoff and Saul Hansell, "Hiding in Plain Sight, Google Seeks More Power," *The New York Times* (June 14, 2006), http://www.nytimes.com/2006/06/14/technology/ 14search.html?_r=1 (accessed July 21, 2009).
8. US Environmental Protection Agency, "Report to Congress on Server and Data Center Energy Efficiency Public Law 109-431," (August 2, 2007), http://www.energystar.gov/ ia/partners/prod_development/downloads/EPA_Datacenter_Report_Congress_Final1. pdf?bcsi_scan_408DE456E3075246=1 (accessed July 21, 2009).
9. IDC, "The Diverse and Exploding Digital Universe," (March 2008), http://www.emc. com/collateral/analyst-reports/diverse-exploding-digital-universe.pdf (accessed July 21, 2009).
10. GSM World, "Market Data Summary," http://www.gsmworld.com/newsroom/market-data/market_data_summary.htm (accessed July 21, 2009).
11. Ibid.
12. Peter Kaplan, "Verizon and AT&T Dominate Airwaves Auction," *Reuters* (March 20, 2008), http://www.reuters.com/article/technologyNews/idUSN2042023420080320?fee dType=RSS&feedName=technologyNews (accessed July 28, 2009).

13. Gartner, "Gartner Says Worldwide Mobile Phone Sales Grew 6 Per Cent in 2008, But Sales Declined 5 Per Cent in the Fourth Quarter" (March 2, 2009), http://www.gartner .com/it/page.jsp?id=904729 (July 21, 2009).

CHAPTER 2: A BRIEF HISTORY OF MODERN TECHNOLOGY

1. Computer History Museum, "First Semiconductor Effect Is Recorded," http://www .computerhistory.org/semiconductor/timeline/1833-first.html (accessed July 21, 2009).
2. Computer History Museum, "Semiconductor Rectifiers Patented as 'Cat's Whisker' Detectors," http://www.computerhistory.org/semiconductor/timeline/1901-semiconductor. html (accessed July 21, 2009).
3. Ibid.
4. Computer History Museum, "1954—Silicon Transistors Offer Superior Operating Characteristics," http://www.computerhistory.org/semiconductor/timeline/1954-Silicon. html (accessed July 21, 2009).
5. Nobelprize.org "The Transistor—Function," http://nobelprize.org/educational_games/ physics/transistor/function/intro.html (accessed July 21, 2009).
6. Intel, "Cramming More Components Onto Integrated Circuits," (April 19, 1965), http://download.intel.com/museum/Moores_Law/Articles-Press_Releases/Gordon_ Moore_1965_Article.pdf (accessed July 21, 2009).
7. Intel, "Our History of Innovation—1968, Intel Corporate Timeline," http://www.intel.com/ museum/corporatetimeline/index.htm?iid=intel_info+rhc_history (accessed July 21, 2009).
8. Intel, "The Intel 4004 Microprocessor," http://www.intel.com/museum/archives/4004facts. htm (accessed July 21, 2009).
9. Ibid.
10. Wade Warner, "Great Moments in Microprocessor History," IBM (December 22, 2004), http://www.ibm.com/developerworks/library/pa-microhist.html (accessed July 21, 2009).
11. Cliff Edwards, "Intel: Supercharging Silicon Valley," *BusinessWeek* (October 4, 2004), http://www.businessweek.com/magazine/content/04_40/b3902032_mz072.htm (accessed July 21, 2009).
12. Patrick Thibodeau, "Obama Lauds Intel Plan to Invest $7B in Chip Plants," *Computer World* (February 10, 2009), http://www.computerworld.com/action/article.do?comman d=viewArticleBasic&articleId=9127708&intsrc=news_ts_head (accessed July 21, 2009).
13. Mary Bellis, "Inventors of the Modern Computer," About.com, http://inventors.about .com/library/weekly/aa060298.htm (accessed July 21, 2009).
14. Computer History Museum, "Timeline of Computer History (1961)," http://www .computerhistory.org/timeline/?category=cmptr (accessed July 21, 2009).
15. Otto Friedrich, "The Computer Moves In," *Time* (January 3 1983), http://www.time. com/time/magazine/article/0,9171,953632-3,00.html (accessed July 21, 2009).
16. Randy Alfred, "April 3, 1973: Motorola Calls AT&T . . . by Cell," Randy Alfred, *Wired* (April 3, 2008), http://www.wired.com/science/discoveries/news/2008/04/dayintech_ 0403 (accessed July 21, 2009).
17. CTIA, "History of Wireless Communications From Building the Wireless Future to Expanding the Wireless Frontier," http://www.ctia.org/media/index.cfm/AID/10390 (accessed July 21, 2009).

18. Symbian Freak, "History of Nokia," (October 19, 2008), http://www.symbian-freak. com/news/008/10/history_of_nokia_corporation.htm (accessed July 21, 2009).

19. National Science Foundation, "The Launch of NSFNET," http://www.nsf.gov/about/ history/nsf0050/internet/launch.htm (accessed July 21, 2009).

20. Ibid.

21. European Organization for Nuclear Research (CERN), "How the Web Began," http://public.web.cern.ch/Public/en/About/WebStory-en.html (accessed July 21, 2009).

22. Free Encyclopedia of Ecommerce, "Internet Service Provider (ISP)—History And Development," http://ecommerce.hostip.info/pages/623/Internet-Service-Provider-ISP-HISTORY-DEVELOPMENT.html (accessed July 21, 2009).

23. Cisco, "Cisco Systems Corporate Timeline," http://newsroom.cisco.com/dlls/time-line/2001_index.shtml (accessed July 21, 2009).

24. Free Encyclopedia of Commerce, "Internet Service Provider (ISP)—Proliferation and Consolidation," http://ecommerce.hostip.info/pages/624/Internet-Service-Provider-ISP-PROLIFERATION-CONSOLIDATION.html (accessed July 21, 2009).

25. Paul Taylor, "Does IT Work?: IT-Related Productivity Gains in Decline," *Financial Times* (October 21, 2008), http://us.ft.com/ftgateway/superpage.ft?news_id=fto 102120081037417526 (accessed July 21, 2009).

26. Kent German, "Top 10 Dot-Com Flops," *CNET*, http://www.cnet.com/1990-11136_ 1-6278387-1.html?tag=cnetfd.sd (accessed July 21, 2009).

27. Source: MSCI. The MSCI information may only be used for your internal use, may not be reproduced or redisseminated in any form, and may not be used to create any financial instruments or products or any indices. The MSCI information is provided on an "as is" basis and the user of this information assumes the entire risk of any use made of this information. MSCI, each of its affiliates, and each other person involved in or related to compiling, computing, or creating any MSCI information (collectively, the "MSCI Parties") expressly disclaims all warranties (including, without limitation, any warranties of originality, accuracy, completeness, timeliness, non-infringement, merchantability, and fitness for a particular purpose) with respect to this information. Without limiting any of the foregoing, in no event shall any MSCI Party have any liability for any direct, indirect, special, incidental, punitive, consequential (including, without limitation, lost profits), or any other damages; Thomson Reuters, as of 3/31/2000 and 3/31/2003.

CHAPTER 3: TECHNOLOGY SECTOR DRIVERS

1. DatacenterDynamics, "Global Vertical Market IT Spending Remains Stable," (February 23, 2009), http://www.datacenterdynamics.com/ME2/dirmod.asp?sid=&nm=&type= news&mod=News&mid=9A02E3B96F2A415ABC72CB5F516B4C10&tier=3&nid= 9510AC6198BA4EE79AF7AD65DBF5A4CD (accessed July 22, 2009).

2. Thomson Reuters.

3. Eric Mah, "Hard-Disk Drive Market Rebounds in 2H07, Says iSuppli," *Digitimes* (November 9, 2007), http://www.digitimes.com/NewsShow/NewsSearch.asp?DocI D=0000000000000000000000000008341&query=HDD+ASP (accessed July 22, 2009).

4. Bloomberg Finance L.P.

5. See note 2.

6. Barry Jaruzelski and Kevin Dehoff, "Beyond Borders: Global Innovation 1000," *strategy+business*, Issue 53 (Winter 2008), http://www.strategy-business.com/press/16635507/08405 (accessed July 22, 2009).

7. World Trade Organization, "Information Technology Agreement—Introduction," http://www.wto.org/english/tratop_E/inftec_e/itaintro_e.htm (accessed July 22, 2009).

8. Ibid.

9. Thomson Reuters, quarterly year-over-year price return data.

10. Source: MSCI. The MSCI information may only be used for your internal use, may not be reproduced or redisseminated in any form, and may not be used to create any financial instruments or products or any indices. The MSCI information is provided on an "as is" basis and the user of this information assumes the entire risk of any use made of this information. MSCI, each of its affiliates, and each other person involved in or related to compiling, computing, or creating any MSCI information (collectively, the "MSCI Parties") expressly disclaims all warranties (including, without limitation, any warranties of originality, accuracy, completeness, timeliness, non-infringement, merchantability, and fitness for a particular purpose) with respect to this information. Without limiting any of the foregoing, in no event shall any MSCI Party have any liability for any direct, indirect, special, incidental, punitive, consequential (including, without limitation, lost profits), or any other damages.

11. Thomson Reuters, Total Return for S&P COMP.

CHAPTER 4: TECHNOLOGY SECTOR BREAKDOWN

1. Source: MSCI. The MSCI information may only be used for your internal use, may not be reproduced or redisseminated in any form, and may not be used to create any financial instruments or products or any indices. The MSCI information is provided on an "as is" basis and the user of this information assumes the entire risk of any use made of this information. MSCI, each of its affiliates, and each other person involved in or related to compiling, computing, or creating any MSCI information (collectively, the "MSCI Parties") expressly disclaims all warranties (including, without limitation, any warranties of originality, accuracy, completeness, timeliness, non-infringement, merchantability, and fitness for a particular purpose) with respect to this information. Without limiting any of the foregoing, in no event shall any MSCI Party have any liability for any direct, indirect, special, incidental, punitive, consequential (including, without limitation, lost profits), or any other damages.

2. Ibid.

3. Ibid.

4. Ibid.

5. Ibid.

6. Ibid.

7. Ibid.

8. Thomson Reuters, MSCI, Inc. as of 12/31/08; MSCI. The MSCI information may only be used for your internal use, may not be reproduced or redisseminated in any form, and may not be used to create any financial instruments or products or any indices. The MSCI information is provided on an "as is" basis and the user of this information assumes the entire risk of any use made of this information. MSCI, each of its affiliates, and each other person involved in or related to compiling, computing, or creating any

MSCI information (collectively, the "MSCI Parties") expressly disclaims all warranties (including, without limitation, any warranties of originality, accuracy, completeness, timeliness, non-infringement, merchantability, and fitness for a particular purpose) with respect to this information. Without limiting any of the foregoing, in no event shall any MSCI Party have any liability for any direct, indirect, special, incidental, punitive, consequential (including, without limitation, lost profits), or any other damages.

9. See note 1.
10. Ibid.
11. See note 9.
12. See note 1.
13. Ibid.
14. Ibid.
15. Ibid.
16. Ibid.
17. See note 1.
18. See note 9.
19. See note 1.
20. See note 1.
21. See note 9.

CHAPTER 5: CHALLENGES IN THE INFORMATION TECHNOLOGY SECTOR

1. IDC, "PC Shipments to Drop 4.5% in 2009, According to IDC," (March 5, 2009), http://www.idc.com/getdoc.jsp?containerId=prUS21725509 (accessed July 21, 2009); "PC Market Continues to Resist Economic Pressures With a Boost From Low Cost Portable PCS, According to IDC," (September 10, 2008), http://www.idc.com/getdoc.jsp?containerId=prUS21420408 (accessed July 21, 2009).
2. SEC, "Apple 1999 10-K," http://www.sec.gov/Archives/edgar/data/320193/0000912057-99-010244.txt, page 10 (accessed July 21, 2009).
3. Apple, "Apple Sells One Millionth iPhone," (September 10, 2007), http://www.apple.com/pr/library/2007/09/10iphone.html (accessed July 21, 2009).
4. Chris Kanaracus, "IDC: Oracle Maintains Lead in Database Market, PC World," *PCWorld* (June 27, 2008), http://www.pcworld.com/businesscenter/article/147684/idc_oracle_maintains_lead_in_database_market.html (accessed July 21, 2009).
5. SEC, "Oracle 1996 10-K," http://www.sec.gov/Archives/edgar/data/777676/0000950109-96-004650.txt (accessed July 22, 2009).
6. Bloomberg Finance L.P.
7. SEC, "Oracle Corporation Annual Filing Form 10-K," (2008), http://www.sec.gov/Archives/edgar/data/1341439/000095013408012257/f41477e10vk.htm (accessed July 22, 2009).
8. Ibid.
9. See note 6.
10. Ibid.
11. Thomson Reuters.
12. IBM, "History of IBM," (1990s), http://www-03.ibm.com/ibm/history/history/decade_1990.html (accessed July 22, 2009).

13. Louis V. Gerstner, "Who Says Elephants Can't Dance?" (Harper Paperbacks, 2002).
14. See note 6.
15. See note 12.
16. See note 13.
17. See note 6.
18. Ibid.
19. Ibid.
20. Ibid.
21. See note 11.
22. Ibid.
23. See note 6.
24. Ibid.
25. Ibid.
26. Bloomberg News, "Software Piracy Cost $53b, Study Says," (May 13, 2009), http://www.boston.com/business/technology/articles/2009/05/13/software_piracy_cost_53b_study_says/ (accessed July 22, 2009).
27. Ibid.

CHAPTER 6: A DEEPER LOOK AT CURRENT & EMERGING TECHNOLOGIES

1. CRC Handbook of Chemistry and Physics and the American Chemical Society, "Silicon," http://periodic.lanl.gov/elements/14.html (accessed July 29, 2009).
2. SEMI, "SEMI Announces Mid-Year Consensus Forecast for Chip Equipment Industry" (July 14, 2008), http://www.semi.org/en/Press/P044189 (accessed July 29, 2009).
3. Ibid.
4. Aaron Hand, "High-Index Lenses Push Immersion Beyond 32 nm," *Semiconductor International* (4/1/2006), http://www.semiconductor.net/article/207786-High_Index_Lenses_Push_Immersion_Beyond_32_nm.php (accessed July 29, 2009).
5. Mark LaPedus, "EUV Woes Fuel Double-Patterning Race," *EE Times* (07/18/2008), http://www.eetimes.com/conf/sw/showArticle.jhtml?articleID=209101258 (accessed July 29, 2009).
6. Aaron Hand, "Double Patterning Battles Cost, Complexity," *Semiconductor International* (7/17/2008), http://www.semiconductor.net/article/203668-Double_Patterning_Battles_Cost_Complexity.php (July 29, 2009).
7. Intel, "Intel's Transistor Technology Breakthrough Represents Biggest Change to Computer Chips In 40 Years" (1/27/07), http://www.intel.com/pressroom/archive/releases/20070128comp.htm (accessed July 29, 2009).
8. Intel, "High-k and Metal Gate Research," http://www.intel.com/technology/silicon/high-k.htm (accessed July 29, 2009).
9. Manek Dubash, "Moore's Law Is Dead, Says Gordon Moore," *Techworld* (April 13, 2005), http://www.techworld.com/opsys/news/index.cfm?newsid=3477 (accessed July 29, 2009).
10. US Environmental Protection Agency, "Nanotechnology: Basic Information," *National Center for Environmental Research*, http://www.epa.gov/ncer/nano/questions/index.html (accessed July 29, 2009).

11. See note 9.
12. eWEEK, "What Is the Difference Between Data Deduplication, File Deduplication, and Data Compression?" (08/15/2007), http://www.eweek.com/c/a/Database/What-Is-the-Difference-Between-Data-Deduplication-File-Deduplication-and-Data-Compression/ (accessed July 29, 2009).

CHAPTER 7: THE TOP-DOWN METHOD

1. Matthew Kalman, "Einstein Letters Reveal a Turmoil Beyond Science," Boston Globe (July 11, 2006), http://www.boston.com/news/world/middleeast/articles/2006/07/11/einstein_letters_reveal_a_turmoil_beyond_science/ (accessed May 9, 2008).
2. Michael Michalko, "Combinatory Play," Creative Thinking, http://www.creativethinking.net/DT10_CombinatoryPlay.htm?Entry=Good (accessed May 9, 2008).
3. Gary P. Brinson, Brian D. Singer, and Gilbert L. Beebower, "Determinants of Portfolio Performance II: An Update," *The Financial Analysts Journal 47* (1991 [3]): 40–48.
4. Source: MSCI. The MSCI information may only be used for your internal use, may not be reproduced or redisseminated in any form and may not be used to create any financial instruments or products or any indices. The MSCI information is provided on an "as is" basis and the user of this information assumes the entire risk of any use made of this information. MSCI, each of its affiliates and each other person involved in or related to compiling, computing or creating any MSCI information (collectively, the "MSCI Parties") expressly disclaims all warranties (including, without limitation, any warranties of originality, accuracy, completeness, timeliness, non-infringement, merchantability and fitness for a particular purpose) with respect to this information. Without limiting any of the foregoing, in no event shall any MSCI Party have any liability for any direct, indirect, special, incidental, punitive, consequential (including, without limitation, lost profits) or any other damages.
5. Ibid.
6. Ibid.
7. Ibid.
8. Ibid.
9. Ibid.

CHAPTER 9: UPGRADING YOUR PORTFOLIO: INVESTING STRATEGIES

1. National Venture Capital Association, "Venture Capital 101: What Is Venture Capital?" http://www.nvca.org/index.php?option=com_docman&task=doc_download&gid=357&Itemid=93 (accessed July 22, 2009).
2. Reuters, "Global Economic Crisis Weighs Heavily on Venture-Backed Exits in 2008," (January 2, 2009), http://www.nvca.org/index.php?option=com_docman&task=doc_download&gid=381&Itemid=317 (accessed July 22, 2009).

About the Authors

Brendan Erne is a global Technology sector equity research analyst at Fisher Investments. He is also a contributing columnist for MarketMinder.com. Brendan received a BA in Finance from Washington State University. Prior to joining Fisher Investments, Brendan worked as a financial advisor for Ameriprise Financial in Bellevue, Washington. Originally from Redmond, Washington, he currently resides in San Francisco.

Andrew S. Teufel (San Francisco, California) has been with Fisher Investments since 1995 where he currently serves as a Co-President and Director of Research. Prior to joining Fisher, he worked at Bear Stearns as a Corporate Finance Analyst in its Global Technology Group. Andrew also instructs at many seminar and educational workshops throughout the US and UK and has lectured at the Haas School of Business at UC Berkeley. He is also the Editor-in-Chief of MarketMinder.com. Andrew is a graduate of UC Berkeley.

Index

Printed and bound by CPI Group (UK) Ltd, Croydon, CR0 4YY

16/04/2025

14658514-0001